THE DBT SKILLS WORKBOOK FOR TEENS

Practical DBT Exercises for Mindfulness, Emotion Regulation, and Distress Tolerance
(2023 Guide for Beginners)

Edric Geis

Contents

Introduction

DBT (Dialectical Behavior Therapy) starts with the premise that "life's challenges are best managed by making adjustments in someone's thoughts and behavior, rather than attempting to get rid of or modify other people, places, or things." "DBT seeks to educate people on how to cope with issues by altering how they think about themselves, others, and the world."

DBT begins with "core beliefs," which are presumed ideas that lead to behaviors that may be difficult or impossible to modify. Beck et al. (1990) defined these underlying ideas as "core irrational beliefs," which include views that life is not worth living that nothing will ever get better, that one is inept and unworthy of aid, and so on. These beliefs are called irrational because they have no basis in reality or cause people to do things that are worse.

DBT is intended to assist individuals in managing the symptoms of mental illness. For those with BPD, a treatment that does not concentrate on the indications of illness (i.e., BPD) but instead focuses on the behaviors indicative of this condition is more beneficial. According to Linehan (1993), "current therapies for BPD are often ineffective because they treat symptoms without addressing the disorder's defining behaviors."

The core belief, also known as an irrational belief, is an assumption about oneself or others that inhibits people with BPD from making significant adjustments in their life. DBT addresses the dysfunctional fundamental beliefs that drive persons with BPD's actions via education and behavioral treatment. DBT therapists may help patients with BPD acquire practical coping strategies for dealing with emotional triggers by assisting them in identifying their basic beliefs. These coping skills will educate children on how to successfully deal with their emotions, eliminate harmful behaviors, and restore balance to their lives.

Cognitive therapy addresses dysfunctional cognitive processes associated with the maladaptive behaviors of people with BPD. Cognitive restructuring means changing a person's bad ideas and wrong beliefs to ease emotional pain and improve behavior.

DBT employs two ways to assist people with BPD in changing maladaptive behaviors. DBT therapists work with their patients to find the core beliefs that are behind their bad behaviors. They then help their patients learn new ways to deal with stress that will change these bad ways of thinking and acting by replacing dysfunctional core beliefs with healthy ones. The new coping abilities are also linked with "procedural learning" behavioral trials in DBT, in which patients are taught how to use these new coping skills in tough settings.

DBT is intended to replace BPD's dysfunctional ways of thinking and acting with more positive and adaptable ones. It has been shown to be effective in treating patients and lowering the number of hospitalizations necessary. It's also been shown to minimize harmful behaviors, including self-injury and suicide ideation. Finally, DBT is beneficial for treating BPD because it is a long-term therapy. In fact, it is the only effective and long-term scientifically validated therapy for BPD.

The Dialectical Behavior Therapy skills model is a four-step interpersonal effectiveness approach that employs a dialectic method. This implies that the abilities build on one another. As one talent is achieved, another builds on it until all four abilities have been mastered.

CHAPTER 1

Basic Distress Tolerance Skills

The DBT Distress Tolerance Skills Module takes into account that some people tend to act in bad ways. It understands that these habits may be overwhelming for such people; thus, they must be handled all at once. Even small amounts of stress can make them feel overwhelmed, so they often pick up bad habits. To aid these individuals, most traditional therapy techniques stress avoiding painful circumstances. However, the goal of the distress intolerance module is to help clients recognize that it is sometimes difficult to prevent discomfort and that the best approach to dealing with such circumstances is to accept things as they are and practice accepting the pain that goes along with them.

The distress tolerance module is based on the notion of radical acceptance. This means that you have to accept the reality of a hard situation and realize that you can't change it. Clients become less sensitive to acquiring persistent, elevated, and powerful negative sensations when they practice radical acceptance without opposing reality or being judgmental.

In DBT, four distinct abilities make up the distress tolerance module. These abilities are intended to assist people in coping with challenging circumstances and experiencing distress without exacerbating the problem. These are as follows:

- Distracting

- Self-soothing

- Improving the situation

- Considering the advantages and disadvantages

Distracting

Distracting the client assists them in shifting their attention away from painful emotions and thoughts and toward neutral or pleasurable activities. It essentially deals with everything that might help you divert yourself from your distress, such as a hobby, a brief stroll in the garden, helping others, or watching a movie. These exercises assist clients in disengaging from an unpleasant environment or a difficult state of mind.

The abbreviation "ACCEPTS" is used to assist people in practicing the art of distraction:

- **Activities:** Positive activities are used to overcome painful circumstances.

- **Contribute:** assist others in your immediate vicinity or in your community.

- **Comparisons:** comparing yourself to individuals who have it worse than you or to yourself at your worst.

- **Emotions:** making oneself feel different by inducing pleasure or humor via appropriate actions.

- **Push away:** temporarily putting your situation in the back of your mind and replacing it with something less stressful.

- **Thoughts:** attempting to ignore what is bothering you and redirecting your attention to other things.

- **Sensations:** doing something severe to give oneself a sensation that is different from the one you are presently experiencing, such as eating a spicy meal or jumping into the shower for a cold bath.

Self-Soothing

The self-soothing program teaches you to appreciate and treat yourself with kindness. It encompasses everything that helps you establish a good picture of yourself using your five senses. For example, looking out the window at a beautiful view (seeing), hearing natural sounds like birds chirping (hearing), burning a fragrant candle (smell), eating a full meal (taste), and caressing an animal are all examples of sensory experiences (touch).

This ability comprises employing self-managed techniques to soothe irritated and agitated customers. In the distress tolerance module of DBT, learning to self-soothe is a crucial milestone. You treat yourself with care, love, and compassion when you self-soothe. This increases your resilience and makes it easier to recover from adversity.

Improving the Situation

The primary goal of this technique is to use positive mental energies to improve your present image in your own eyes. This talent may be honed by remembering the acronym IMPROVE.

- **Imagery:** Imagery entails envisioning something that soothes you in order to dissolve bad ideas.

- **Meaning:** Meaning entails drawing meaning or purpose from suffering or a tough circumstance. Simply said, it is all about looking for the silver lining in whatever you do. This assists the customer in finding optimism in all situations and in learning something new.

- **Prayer:** Prayer entails asking God for strength and confidence. Many customers find that prayer strengthens their spiritual side and helps them to calm down.

- **Relaxation:** Relaxation is relaxing your physical body and tensed muscles via activities such as listening to music, sipping warm milk, or receiving a massage.

- **One thing at the moment:** urging the person to be aware and focused on a neutral activity taking place in the present.

- **Vacation:** This involves helping people to take a mental vacation from a challenging circumstance by picturing or doing something nice. It might be anything, such as going on a vacation or ignoring all phone calls for a time.

- **Encouragement:** Encouragement is having a helpful and pleasant dialogue with oneself to get through a difficult time.

In ideal situations, the IMPROVE skill lets clients endure annoyance or distress without worsening things. It is especially for those who are in dismal circumstances that are beyond their control. These individuals are powerless to change these fundamental problems and hence feel helpless, wounded, and discouraged. For many individuals, such a circumstance may seem like a never-ending crisis; therefore, using IMPROVE skills will help them move through it and restore confidence.

Considering the Pros and Cons

With this ability, you are generally required to compile a list of all the benefits of accepting a stressful situation and weigh them against the disadvantages of not tolerating it (i.e., dealing with it via self-destructive behaviors). The key aim is to assist them in recalling how avoiding confrontation in tough circumstances in the past harmed them and to let them comprehend how it will feel to be able to bear present stress without developing harmful habits. This assists patients in reducing impulsive responses.

Make a list of the benefits and drawbacks of acting on your urges. Participating in destructive, addictive, or risky activities, as well as giving in, giving up, or just postponing what has to be done, are all examples of acting on your impulses.

Make a separate list of the advantages and disadvantages of rejecting certain wants. Carry your list with you at all times and go over it regularly. If you are in a crisis situation or driven to act quickly, refer to your list. Examine what happened when you followed your instincts in a crisis.

This time, utilize your list of benefits and drawbacks to help you decide on a new course of action.

Summary

The distress tolerance skills taught as part of DBT are primarily concerned with coping with the suffering and pain unavoidable in human life. The client's distress tolerance skill gives them useful tools to assist them in keeping their senses and equilibrium in stressful situations. Instead of developing negative habits, it teaches kids to accept better and manage their distress. Following it helps clients learn how to connect truthfully with others, be open to their emotions, and adapt flexibly to life's ups and downs.

Clients may weather any uncomfortable time and lessen destructive impulses and painful sensations by learning how to divert themselves, better their present moments, self-soothe their minds and body, and balance the advantages and cons of a given scenario. It will allow them to take a break and return to life calmer, invigorated, and more focused, like a full gas tank that can now travel for miles.

CHAPTER 2

Advanced Distress Tolerance Skills

Advanced Distress Tolerance, One of the most significant parts of emotional intelligence skills. This is because they help you deal with your thoughts and feelings in a healthy way instead of letting them run your life.

At the end of the day, your opinions are your views, not facts. Your emotions are not facts; they are just your emotions. You get to determine what you think of them.

You can only fully control yourself when you learn to make logical, sensible decisions based on what you know and how you feel. The more talents you have, the better your chances of dealing with any scenario and controlling your emotions and moods. These ten fundamentally advanced talents in distress tolerance are critical.

1. Determine your course of action.

This tool focuses on taking action to improve the issue. For example, if you are in an awkward social situation, you would utilize this talent to get out of it or get through it faster. Perhaps you're on the highway and get trapped in traffic. This ability will allow you to reach home quicker.

What's vital to understand is that taking action is only effective when the next step in your goal's progression is evident. If you know you need to make a decision (large or small), this is a skill that may assist.

2. Identify the issue

This talent is all about identifying the issue and then solving it. For example, it might be beneficial to sit down and identify your anxiety if you suffer from it. Then you'll be able to devise a solution to assist you in dealing with it in the long term.

3. Identify your own assets.

This ability is all about identifying your own particular talents. It entails getting to know yourself and your flaws. The more you understand yourself, the better you can anticipate what you will do in certain scenarios. This can help you figure out how you will act in certain situations or what feelings you will have.

4. Divert your attention

This is one of the most prevalent Advanced Distress Tolerance Skills that individuals are unaware they possess. This distraction technique helps relieve stress and anxiety by taking your mind off of things that make you feel bad. For example, watching a hilarious YouTube video might be beneficial if you're going through a difficult period. This will help you divert your attention away from your worry or anxiety.

5. Concentrate on the positive

Focusing on the good parts of a situation can help you feel better about it, which is part of this skill. For example, if you're having a difficult time with your employer, it might be beneficial to concentrate on all of the good things in your life. Perhaps you're thinking about a new work opportunity. Maybe you're aiming for something huge in life. Your daughter may be doing well in school. Even if things seem to be going in the wrong direction, concentrate on the positive to make yourself feel better.

6. Develop pleasant feelings

This technique is all about cultivating happy feelings by focusing on happiness. It would help if you had a feeling of success and purpose in life to keep your optimism alive and your fear at bay.

7. Make yourself feel better

This ability is all about making yourself feel better by taking action to get the greatest potential result. For example, if you're having a terrible time at work, it might be beneficial to ask yourself what you can do to get out of it. If you don't receive a response, it's OK to act on your own.

8. Make a contribution

This talent is all about positively contributing by assisting others and making a difference in the world around you. Maybe you may give to a charity or create your own. Perhaps you can volunteer and make a difference in the lives of others.

9. Create a new plan

This ability helps you make new strategies and escape from old circumstances by devising new solutions to issues. For example, making a new strategy might be beneficial if you're worried about your work. Maybe you want to start your own company or return to school. This is all about making plans for the future.

10. Be inspired

This talent is all about getting motivated by other people's success stories, such as reading books, watching motivational films, or visiting motivational websites. For example, if you're going through a terrible moment in your life, it might be beneficial to check for a motivational video online. Perhaps you'll come across a speech from someone who has been where you are and succeeded.

These abilities are not confined to stress or worry. They may help with any mental distress you may regularly have. You can manage emotional distress in any form with the aid of these tools and techniques. The more sophisticated your plan, the more successful it may be.

You will discover that various challenges require distinct methods. These ten fundamental skills are all about developing the best plan for dealing with difficulties. As you begin to use them, you will realize how useful they are in daily life. You'll get better at using them in all parts of your life over time, which will help you deal with emotional stress well.

I'm certain that once you've mastered these Advanced Distress Tolerance Skills, they will serve as the basis for all future triumphs.

CHAPTER 3

More Distress Tolerance Skills

Everyone has been in an awkward situation, whether it's being stopped in traffic, being late for work, or running out of coffee on their way to work.

At some time in our life, we all suffer greater sadness and anguish, such as the end of a marriage, the death of a close relative, or the loss of a job.

Some persons, especially those with borderline personality disorder (BPD), are more prone than others to suffer extreme pain as a result of these situations. In fact, individuals may feel an intolerable sense of loss that seems to emanate from the inside and has little to do with what is happening around them.

People with BPD who have not yet learned to deal with their distress via appropriate coping mechanisms may develop unhealthy habits such as self-harm, drug misuse, or other poor impulse control that seem to give a fast "cure." Still, these behaviors may increase the pain in the long term.

DBT teaches vulnerable people to distress tolerance skills that help them handle challenging or unpleasant situations and control their desire to participate in harmful behaviors.

When Should DBT Distress Tolerance Skills Be Used to Survive a Crisis?

- When someone is in extreme physical and emotional pain, that isn't going away any time soon.

- An individual's urge to act on emotions will only exacerbate issues.

Despite the enormous nature of the issue, certain necessities must be met. Someone is very driven or determined to address an issue that cannot be solved right now. However, it is vital not to use these crisis survival abilities to deal with daily issues or all of the problems that may come during your life. Only apply crisis survival skills when confronted with a crisis situation.

If you wish to modify an event or an emotion, you must use a different set of DBT strategies called emotional regulation skills.

Distress Tolerance DBT STOP Skill

The STOP skill is an excellent first-aid tool in a crisis.

- **"S" stands for "Stop:"** which means that you should not respond to any stimuli that come your way. Maintain control over both your emotions and your physical body. Maintain as much stillness as possible.

- **Take a deep breath:** and step back! The greatest thing you can do is remove yourself from the situation. Take a large breath or a brief break. Don't make impulsive decisions based on your emotions.

- **Observe:** pay attention! Take some time to observe your surroundings and environment, both inside and out. What are your opinions? What are others' behaviors and words?

- **Proceed with caution:** assess your current aims and behave with total awareness. What activities can you take to help the situation, and which will make it worse?

Make yourself your best cheerleader. "You got this," "I'll be OK," or "You're the guy!" tell yourself.

DBT TIPP Skill

DBT Skill TIPP is unique because of its physiological nature. You can change your thoughts by changing your body chemistry. It is one of the most efficient ways to calm down powerful emotions quickly.

- "T" Put your face in a pail of ice water or use a ziplock bag full of ice to apply ice to your forehead, cheeks, temples, and eyes.

- "I" Intense exercise: focus all of your emotions' stored physical energy into something physically demanding, such as running, lifting weights, or engaging in a sport. Work up a decent sweat.

- "P" Paced breathing means slowing down your breathing. For even longer lengths of time, inhale deeply through your nose and exhale thoroughly through your mouth. Focus. Inhale for at least five seconds before exhaling for seven. Practice for as long as you believe it is necessary.

- "P" Pairing muscle relaxation: Tense your body muscles as you breathe. Make a mental note of how tense the situation is. Notice how your body transforms when you breathe and remove the tension.

Begin with only your legs or arms and work your way up to other muscle groups.

Cold Water DBT Skill

Cold water is another excellent physiological strategy to use in an emergency. Submerge your face in cold water for 15 to 30 seconds. Your brain responds in a method known as the "dive reaction." In other words, your brain believes you're drowning. To manage and safeguard your body, your brain slows your pulse. The flow of blood to your extremities is slowed, and blood is diverted to the vital components of your heart and brain.

Distress Tolerance for Anger Management

When you feel an emotion so deeply that you are outside your "window of tolerance" and cannot engage in your emotion management abilities, Dialectical Behavioral Therapy employs distress tolerance approaches. You won't be able to check the facts if you're so outraged that you can't think clearly. To begin, you must relax using strategies for distress tolerance.

In Dialectical Behavioral Therapy, Distress Tolerance is a fundamental skills module. As a result, there are numerous talents to use. Mindfulness practices, such as counting breaths while breathing deeply into your diaphragm or truthfully describing your surroundings and the various items you observe around you, are instances of distress tolerance.

Distraction may be a great technique for distress tolerance when used sparingly and wisely. Distraction is described as any activity that diverts your attention away from extreme emotion, such as cleaning the dishes, watching a funny show, or going for a stroll.

Another example of the talent in distress tolerance is self-soothing. Self-soothing is a method of relaxing your emotions by concentrating on your senses. Self-soothing activities include drinking a cup of tea or coffee, applying your favorite scented lotion, gazing out the window at the trees, petting your dog, or listening to your favorite music.

Radical Acceptance

There will undoubtedly be instances in your life when you are unable to alter your circumstances. You may strongly dislike or disapprove of it, which just adds to your distress. You may decrease the distress you experience and be at peace with yourself if you just accept it for what it is. If you stop obsessing about the problem or condition, you may simply move on.

Radical acceptance is a basic skill that thinks we all have options and that sometimes the only choice you have is whether or not to embrace the truth of a circumstance. You have the option to rant about the problem and be unhappy as a result of it. You may also choose to accept it and move on. For example, suppose you have a cavity but are afraid of going to the dentist. You may attempt to avoid it, dismiss it, or even deny its existence. You had a wonderful connection with the other dentist, but he retired. The new dentist does not seem to be understanding, and you dislike them. To prevent visits to the dentist, you begin by removing your favorite foods that aggravate the cavities, such as all sweet delights. It works out well for you since you are now consuming fewer bad foods. However, the hollow flares up every now and again, producing excruciating agony.

When you practice radical acceptance, you get the fortitude to accept that you are afraid of going to the dentist and that it will most likely be an unpleasant experience. However, it also gives you the confidence to realize that you must get the hole filled. With radical acceptance, you accept the worst and move on from experience. It is not simple to learn distress tolerance abilities, but it is worthwhile.

CHAPTER 4

Basic Mindfulness Skills

Mindfulness is defined as having a knowledgeable mind and being present in the present moment. Being conscious has several elements. It entails watching, describing, and taking part in the current moment. What does doing these things imply? It means not allowing your thoughts to wander. Return to the current moment.

Even if you don't have BPD or any other documented mental illness, understanding mindfulness and how to live in the now without worrying about the future or the past is a valuable skill.

Mindfulness is a fundamental psychotherapy approach that may be used to address anxiety, anger, sadness, and other psychological issues. While it originates in eastern mysticism, western science has done much research on the issue. Psychotherapists even recommend mindfulness meditation for those suffering from certain mental health issues. Mindfulness training is essential to CBT, DBT, and ACT (Acceptance and Commitment Therapy). In fact, it is one of DBT's four skill modules.

Mindfulness is a state of mind that may be reached by concentrating our attention on what is occurring in the present moment. It also entails accepting our emotions, experiences, and ideas calmly.

For some, the difficulty of concentrating on the present moment may seem easy, yet it is really easier said than done. Our minds might wander, we can lose touch with the present moment, and we can get immersed in compulsive thoughts about the past or worry about the future. However, no matter how far our minds wander from the present, we may employ mindfulness to return to what we are doing or experiencing quickly.

Even though it is natural for us to be attentive whenever we want, we may grow mindfulness further with powerful ACT practices that you will discover later.

Typically, meditation and mindfulness are associated. While meditation may help you attain mindfulness, there is more to it than that. Mindfulness is a kind of being present that may be used at any moment. It is a state of awareness that may be attained by consciously focusing on the present moment without judgment.

Elements of Mindfulness

The two basic components of mindfulness are attention and attitude.

Attention

Many of us suffer from what is described as the "monkey mind," when the mind acts like a monkey hanging from one branch to another. Our brains may wander away and then return, and we typically have no clue how we end up thinking about anything.

The monkey mind is often preoccupied with the past, obsessing over what has occurred or what you believe might have occurred if you had done differently. It also leans toward the future, concerned about what could happen. The experience of the present moment will be stolen if the monkey mind is fed. Focusing your attention on what is occurring right now is what mindfulness is all about, remember.

Attitude

Mindfulness is based on the ideals of compassion and judgment suspension. As a result, a really aware person understands how to accept reality and refrains from disputing it. This may seem like a simple chore, but if you practice mindfulness, you will become aware of how often we evaluate ourselves and our thoughts.

Here are some statements that we use to judge ourselves and others:

- I'm not very good at this.

- My clothing is hideous.

- I dislike my surroundings.

- I despise my next-door neighbor.

- What a sour waitress.

Mindfulness is also the practice of quieting our inner critic. It enables us to let go of our internal expectations and embrace how things are in the current moment. However, keep in mind that this does not imply you are not required to make the necessary modifications. Remember that you merely defer your judgment to give yourself more time to think about the problem and take action. The fundamental distinction is that you may make adjustments when you are in a perfect frame of mind for change rather than when you are impacted by tension or stress.

Furthermore, mindfulness will help you to be more sympathetic to yourself, embrace your experience, and care for others. You may retrain your brain to be nicer and more compassionate as you practice mindfulness.

How Mindfulness Can Reshape Your Brain

People used to assume that the human brain could only grow to a certain point, generally between early infancy and puberty. Various studies, however, have proven that our brain can rearrange itself by creating neuronal connections. This is known as neuroplasticity, and it has no bounds.

Neuroscientists have debunked the long-held idea that the human brain is a static, unchanging organ. They revealed that the human brain could compensate for damage caused by age, sickness, or accident by reconstructing itself. Simply stated, our brain has the ability to heal itself.

Studies have also shown mindfulness to aid in the growth of the brain. It especially aids in the neuroplasticity process. It's incredible to realize that neuroplasticity and mindfulness allow us to alter our emotions, feelings, and mental processes.

Three important studies demonstrate how neuroplasticity, which is a component of mindfulness, may reorganize the human brain.

Mindfulness Can Improve Memory, Learning, and Other Cognitive

Functions

Even though mindfulness meditation is associated with physical relaxation and tranquillity, practitioners argue that the practice may also aid in learning and memory.

Sara Lazar, a Harvard University Medical School professor, developed an 8-week mindfulness-based meditation program. She performed the program with a team of Massachusetts General Hospital researchers to investigate the relationship between mindfulness and cognitive function improvement.

The program included weekly meditation sessions and audio recordings for the 16 volunteers who meditated independently. Meditation was performed for an average of 27 minutes by the participants. For study purposes, the basic premise of mindfulness meditation was to achieve a state of mind in which individuals suspend their judgment and just concentrate on sensing sensations.

Later, the scientists employed Magnetic Resonance Imaging (MRI) to obtain pictures of the subjects' brain structures. An MRI scan was also requested of a group of people who were not meditating (the control group).

The researchers were astounded by the outcome. The research participants first reported that they had considerable cognitive benefits, as shown by their replies to the mindfulness survey. In addition, an MRI scan revealed detectable physical variations in the density of gray matter, which the researchers confirmed.

Gray matter density in the amygdala, the brain region responsible for stress and anxiety, was reduced. Significant alterations were seen in the brain regions involved in self-awareness, introspection, and compassion. Gray matter density was enhanced in the hippocampus, the area of the brain responsible for memory and learning.

According to this Harvard research, neuroplasticity may play an active part in brain growth through practicing meditation. It is great to know that we can do something daily to enhance our quality of life and general well-being.

Mindfulness Can Help Combat Depression

Depression affects millions of individuals worldwide. For example, around 19 million individuals in the United States seek medicine to treat depression. This is around 10% of the total US population.

Dr. Zindel Segal, a Psychiatry Professor at the University of Toronto, utilized a MacArthur Foundation research grant to investigate mindfulness's benefits in treating depression. The research, which was primarily focused on the delivery of mindfulness-based stress reduction sessions, was deemed a success, and he did follow-up research to investigate the usefulness of mindfulness meditation in depressed patients. As a consequence, Mindfulness-Based Cognitive Therapy, or MBCT, was developed.

The research included individuals who were depressed, with 8 out of 10 experiencing at least three episodes. Compared to those prescribed alternative therapy, such as antidepressants, around 30% of individuals who suffered at least three bouts of depression did not return for more than a year after the stress reduction sessions.

Segal's research has served as a model for studies supported by Oxford and Cambridge Universities in the United Kingdom, with comparable results. The study has been very useful in establishing mindfulness meditation as an effective and healthier alternative to medicine in the United Kingdom. It has also persuaded mental health practitioners to recommend mindfulness meditation to their patients.

Mindfulness meditation and MBCT research investigations are progressively gaining traction in medical and scientific circles in the United States and other areas of the world.

Mindfulness Can Help in Stress Relief

According to research, even 25 minutes a day of mindfulness might reduce stress. Prof. David Creswell headed the research, which included 66 people aged 18 to 30.

For three days, one set of research participants required a brief meditation practice consisting of 25 minutes of mindfulness. This group was instructed to do certain exercises aimed at training them to focus on their breathing while shifting their attention to the present moment.

The second group utilized the same time period to evaluate poetry readings to enhance their problem-solving abilities.

During the assessment phase, all participants were required to perform math and speaking problems in front of stern examiners. All participants reported elevated stress levels and were asked to provide saliva samples to assess levels of the stress hormone cortisol.

It's worth noting that the same group had greater stress hormone levels, something the researchers didn't anticipate. The study showed that when individuals practice mindfulness meditation, they must actively engage in the technique, especially under stress. Despite a higher cortisol level, the cognitive work may seem less stressful to the person.

To make the mindfulness sessions less stressful and lower cortisol levels, the team is currently concentrating on automating them. However, it is obvious that short-term meditation may significantly reduce stress even in the early stages.

Other Benefits of Mindfulness

Aside from the advantages mentioned earlier, mindfulness meditation significantly impacts our emotional, mental, and physical health.

We can be more empathetic thanks to mindfulness. Those who practice mindfulness meditation have changes in certain brain regions linked to empathy. It also reduces our emotional sensitivity. According to research done at Massachusetts General Hospital, mindfulness lowers the size of the amygdala, which is responsible for fear, anxiety, and aggressiveness.

Mindfulness meditation may help us avoid negative ideas, which our brain is prone to when left to its own devices. The research was done in 2007 among students who were taught meditation techniques. It was discovered that mindfulness assisted pupils in increasing their concentration and decreasing self-doubt, anxiety, and sadness. In schools where mindfulness sessions were promoted, there was also a considerable drop in suspensions and absences.

Mindfulness is also being utilized to treat anxiety and depression symptoms. Many psychotherapists now recommend mindfulness meditation to patients experiencing depressive episodes.

CHAPTER 5

Advanced Mindfulness Skills

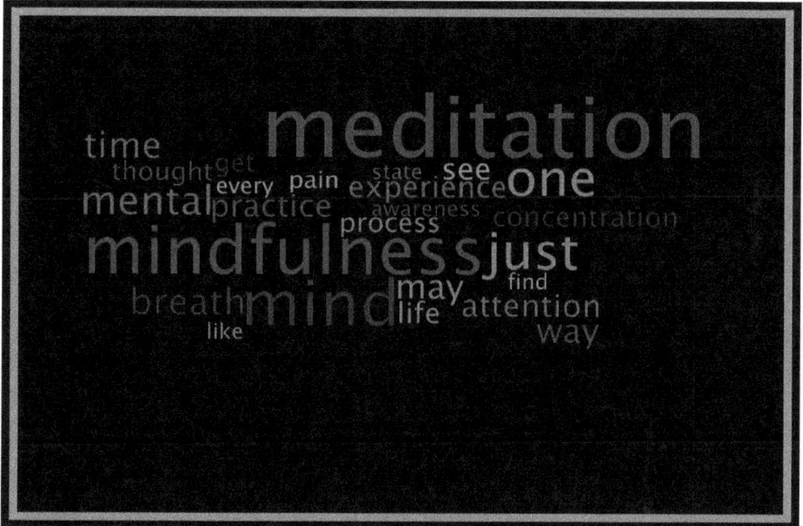

If you've heard much about mindfulness meditation, trust it; it's genuine. People who practice mindful meditation are said to have more tolerance, contentment, compassion, and acceptance in their life. They also have reduced degrees of annoyance, tension, and depression.

Are you still not convinced? Here are some study findings that support this.

- Various research investigations conducted by North-eastern University indicated that participating in three weeks of Headspace mindfulness meditation increased compassion by 23% and reduced animosity by 57%.

- In research involving ten students, it was discovered that mindfulness meditation boosted their positivity and well-being.

The Aspects of Mindfulness

- Patience is allowing things to blossom in their own time and letting go of the need to control things in order to achieve a desired result.

- Believe in yourself. Our experiences are real and allow us to identify ourselves based on our past experiences. It assists us in distinguishing between what is false and what is true. It's all about trusting your instincts.

- Because the experience happens in the present moment, acceptance and appreciation foster openness and goodwill toward it. It's not about being passive but about accepting that things are as they are. Resistance to it might lead to tension and worry.

- Gratitude encourages us to focus our attention on the good in our life rather than becoming trapped or wallowing in the bad.

Mindfulness in DBT

As you may have guessed, mindfulness plays a significant role in Dialectical Behavior Modification. It is one of the fundamental abilities that underpin all of the talents taught in DBT.

Mindfulness is one of the main things taught to the patient or client in a DBT session. Long-standing habits of emotions, action and thinking are unlikely to be initiated without mindfulness.

Therapists use DBT to demonstrate and impart awareness to patients to help them learn to control emotions, effectively resolve interpersonal disputes, and get through crises without increasing panic. Mindfulness is also an important part of understanding the notion of the Wise Mind. DBT's Wise Mind idea integrates our Reasonable Mind and Emotion Mind. The Wise Mind allows us to recognize what is genuine and real, allowing us to make better judgments about how to respond and react.

Mindfulness is not a complex philosophy. It's almost like learning to be conscious, and all you need to do is be dedicated. Being aware is saying YES to being present in the current moment.

Now that you have a clear understanding of what mindfulness is, we'll look at how it's often provided via DBT on a daily basis. You'll discover what to do to practice mindfulness and how to try it via DBT. These are known as "What" and "How" abilities.

The "What" Skills

In DBT, these three skills are performed one at a time and utilize the "What" part of mindfulness.

- Observe

- Describe

- Participate

The "How" Skills

The "How" component of mindfulness consists of these three abilities. The "How" skills direct how you use the "What" abilities, and they are trained together:

- Nonjudgmentally

- One-mindfully

- Effectively

After practicing mindfulness in DBT, what should one do? You basically observe, describe, and participate. To be effective in observing, describing, and participating, you must be of one mind and not be judgmental.

The Observe Skill in Mindfulness

The Observe talent is all about recognizing and being aware of any direct sensory sensations. It is about experiencing, seeing, tasting, touching, and hearing without naming those sensations, not responding to them, and not judging them.

It may be tough or confusing for many individuals to travel through this without reacting or putting on any labels, but you'll ultimately teach yourself to possess naked feelings during a certain encounter.

By committing to practicing the Observe skill, you allow instantaneous experiences to take place without attempting to change circumstances or push the experience away.

This talent, like all others, is learned via practice. This often implies that academic comprehension isn't enough—you need to experience it to really embody what it means.

The Observe mindfulness skill may be practiced with the following exercises:

- Pay attention to the noises around you, taking careful note of what you hear without adding any remarks.

- Pay attention to your breathing by studying the feelings of inhalation and expiration, the rise and fall of your abdomen as you inhale and exhale.

- You may also sit on a seat and observe the goods and people passing immediately in front of you without reacting, categorizing, or moving your head.

Observe abilities are important for allowing you to be present in the moment, to feel alive inside the time you're in, and to avoid being caught in your thoughts of previous experiences or future expectations.

Thanks to the Observe talent, you are HERE and NOW and nowhere else. You are experiencing reality as it is. When you awaken to what is in every moment, you become more focused, peaceful, and alert; notice, and you have a greater inclination to apply your Wise Mind.

The Describe Skill in Mindfulness

The Describe skill is an extension of the Observe skill. While the Observe skill introduces you to the concept of attention, which is observing without labels, the Explain talent allows you to do exactly what it says—describe the observation, or describe what you observe in Observe based on your experiences, emotions, or ideas.

The difficult aspect would be practicing the Describe skill in DBT without adding your own assumptions and interpretations. As you explain the situations you perceive, you assign a label to each one. So, by labeling emotions as feelings, senses as sensations, and thoughts as ideas, you are not adding factors such as your own views, assumptions, judgments, or notions.

This Describe talent is useful for ensuring that you do not confuse every sensation or notion with a fact. For example, just because you feel like a loser doesn't imply it's true. This technique might help you reduce negative thoughts, particularly if you are emotionally sensitive.

The Describe skill allows you to avoid reacting rashly or jumping to conclusions based on incomplete information. It may also aid or prevent you from obsessing over unimportant or bad ideas without first examining the facts. Fact-checking before leaping to conclusions or letting your thoughts run wild may help you in a variety of ways. For one thing, you won't be agitated, your head won't be crowded with bad ideas, and you won't be dalliance and waste energy on unimportant things. You may also ask questions during fact-checking. Here's an example of the Observe skill in action:

You go out for drinks with a lover and start conversing. You bring them up in order to urge them to speed up with what's going on in your life, and you see that they keep getting sidetracked. The negative mentality would cause you to get irritated and lash out at them for "ignoring" you. However, the DBT Observe mind would inquire as to what is wrong and seek out what is occupying their thoughts, why they seem preoccupied, and what is upsetting them.

This not only avoids a conflict but also helps you to sympathize with one another. It will lead you to ask them why they are preoccupied. You'll find yourself looking around more; maybe they're looking about it but don't want to talk about it.

By not believing your assessment of the facts, the Observe mind has spared you a lot of avoidable pain.

The Participate Skill in Mindfulness

Participate talent is all about being a part of and completely interested in a certain activity. It also entails letting go of preconceived notions, self-consciousness, and anxiety. You're not just sitting on the sidelines with the Participate skill. You're a gang member, a part of a movement, and you're completely immersed in the whole event.

The Participate skill will appear different depending on the activity. Here are a few such examples:

You are taking part in a group team-building exercise. Most people are waiting for someone else to talk. You consider things, believe in what you want to say, and contribute by being the one to talk and give suggestions. The rest of the group follows suit, making it easy to share ideas.

You go into a salsa dancing club where everyone is having a good time. You're a little apprehensive, but after a few minutes, a salsa dancer approaches you and asks you to bop. You let go of your inhibitions and join the dancers on the floor, completely surrendering to the sensation of the noises, lights, motions, music, and hence rhythm without thinking about how you appear.

You join a tour group and sample the local food. Everyone else at the party is hesitant to try this new dish, but you delve in, completely immersing yourself in the experience.

It is all about the experience when you participate. It's not about the quality of your work; rather, it's about the quality of your experience. Fully immersing oneself in a particular event or experience does not suggest that you are superior to others who did not try, taste, or dance. It just implies you're having fun, not worrying what others think of you, and you'll have a great time participating in the event.

CHAPTER 6

Exploring Mindfulness Further

Practicing Mindfulness Meditation

Understanding what mindfulness is and how it connects to meditation is beneficial. Strong knowledge of this may aid you in developing a set of routines and habits that you may follow to help you reduce your anxiety and stress. Being attentive entails being aware of where you are, what you are doing, and what you want to attempt to be completely involved in the here and now. It's a condition in which you're neither distracted nor judged. You are aware of your emotions and ideas but are not obsessed with them.

We teach ourselves to be aware of every waking moment through meditation practice. We improve our mindfulness abilities throughout this freeing exercise so that it becomes a habit in our everyday lives. We become anchored in this present by training our thoughts and teaching ourselves to engage with everything in life with mindfulness. As a result, we live more completely, breathing deliberately and without feeling obligated to some sensitive sentiments and ideas. This perspective enables us to tackle some of life's most unpleasant, stressful, and trying situations.

Am I attentive at any given moment without even realizing it?

Typically, researchers employ a standard questionnaire to measure participants' mindfulness. The Mindful Attention Awareness Score (MAAS) is offered to persons who want to learn more about themselves regarding awareness and mindfulness.

If you obtained a high score, this indicates that you are typically awake and mindful. But don't worry if your score is lower than you expected.

Mindfulness requires practice in the same way that meditation and everything else you want to be excellent at need practice. If you got a lower score, it means you'd benefit from some mindfulness meditation techniques.

You'll be better able to manage stress, improve your energy, deepen your compassion and concentration, and increase empathy and patience if you practice mindfulness meditation. If you're new to meditation and mindfulness, working with an instructor, using an app like Headspace, or watching YouTube videos would all be good places to start.

This book may help you immerse and internalize mindfulness by providing clarification on concepts you don't understand and introducing a sequence of tasks that will help you improve your practice.

There are several mindfulness techniques available today. Each of them has origins in a certain tradition or teaching technique, as well as specific expertise in a specific philosophy. Whatever way you choose; these strategies all have one thing in common: they all have a single point of concentration. They're all intended to reinforce and strengthen a couple of key areas—calmness and clarity—with the single goal of keeping focused and aware.

Meditation

Meditation, also known as metacognition, is the act of reflecting on one's own thoughts. How to work with your mind is what this mindfulness practice entails. Mindfulness mostly involves the mind. Meditation helps you to start building a framework around what mindfulness entails. You must be willing to take a step back and think about your ideas and feelings. They might be tales, stories, or memories from your past. So you have a continuing commentary and interpretation of the events that are repeating themselves in your mind, in addition to the recollection of the event.

Meditation enables you to absorb the characteristics of your ideas. It informs you of the sort of thoughts you're thinking and helps you to begin taking inventory and noticing thought patterns in your life. It helps you to go back during the day and observe your mind's inner chatter, allowing you to begin to detect the sort of ideas you're having and put a spin on them. Your ideas have a distinct taste and attitude. They have the property that, regardless of the context, another sub-communication will exist underneath it.

Meditation enables you to examine how you are telling yourself the tale of your day. You may begin to realize that your thoughts are furious, and the quality of your mind associated with the ideas is erratic. You may begin to notice a reoccurring pattern that causes you to experience rage, jealousy, fear, or concern. You may not always have thoughts based on anger, fear, or concern; you may have periods when your thoughts move from fear to anger based on resentment, fear to confidence, or worry to delight.

You'll have this neutral sense where you'll feel satisfied at times. You will not experience mood swings at such times. You will not feel warm, tenderhearted, or energetically aroused; instead, you will feel indifferent. So you're transforming ideas that are based on concerns or anxieties into neutral ones. You'll be able to map out, distinguish, and classify the quality of your ideas if you take the time to engage with your mind and approach it from a meta-perspective. You may begin to deal with the shift and gaps in your mind when you are not in your recurring habitual thinking. Simply paying attention to what you see in the here and now is what mindfulness is all about.

When you look within yourself and begin to feel, experience, and absorb what you perceive in your mind, you are just charting your mental state. You're not attempting to influence or alter them. You're not attempting to make people feel wonderful, warm, and cuddly, nor are you attempting to reduce those feelings; instead, you're adopting a very neutral observing posture and explaining your thoughts in the same way that a scientist or journalist would describe an occurrence. You attempt to take a step back and get a birds-eye perspective of your thoughts.

Paced Breathing

Because mindfulness is all about being in the present moment, concentrating on your breath is one of the finest methods to practice and bring yourself into the present moment.

Slowing your breathing may also assist to relax your nervous system, quieting your thoughts, reducing your heart rate, and manage your powerful emotions. Slowing your breathing creates a whole-system reaction, which is what occurs when you feel emotions.

When you feel emotions, your whole body responds, so if you can modify your breathing in reaction to those feelings, you may push yourself to be more likely to change that mood. If you want to modify it, embrace it, or just be able to react to it more generally.

The Paced Breathing Cycle

Sit comfortably erect with your feet firmly planted on the ground to prepare for focused breathing. Maintain a straight and comfortable back. Place your hands on your thighs, and either lay up or down softly. Keep your eyes open and gaze down at a single point.

It would be best if you inhaled gently through your nose when you began your breathing cycle. When you breathe in deeply, push out your stomach so that you're filling up your stomach with air, much like you'll do to a balloon. Use your diaphragm for breathing. You will experience deeper and more complete breathing when you breathe in through your belly. In addition, inhale gently into your abdomen and then naturally pause when your lungs are full of air. Now exhale slowly and deeply through your nose, pushing the air out of your belly as much as possible, and after you've completely released all the air, pause naturally again and resume the cycle.

As you begin to practice paced breathing, attempt to increase the duration of your inhale and exhale intervals with each breath. So, after taking a big breath, stop and exhale. Try to breathe out a little bit farther each time you breathe in and out to extend your breath. Also, try to calm your breathing to a comfortable, regular pace; while inhaling, make sure it's steady and inwards. As you attempt to gain control of your breathing, make sure it's even. There will be a graph that you may follow while you practice the mindful activity; you don't have to match it precisely; it's just there for you to utilize and see how long you'd want your breathing to be. Use it as a guide. Pay attention to your own thoughts and body. It may be used as a guide to practice timed breathing.

As you finish the mindfulness exercise, make a mental note of your thoughts and emotions. Were the ideas pleasant or unpleasant, and were they intrusive? Make a mental note of whatever it is.

CHAPTER 7

Basic Emotion Regulation Skills

The capacity to manage emotions and emotional reactions are called emotional regulation. The interest in this concept stems from the hypothesis that it is connected to adaptive ways of mental functioning since deficiencies in this area are associated with various types of mental distress. Numerous awareness techniques include training on the difference between emotion and behavior. Some of them emphasize controlling and suppressing negative emotions, proposing opposing them and relying on good emotions. At the same time, acceptance of all feelings as they emerge, suspending only the development of the chain of responses and dysfunctional behavior, is more often stressed. This unusual viewpoint departs from established therapeutic methods to care and intervention in that the goal of transforming the feeling is not prioritized, but rather "staying in it," "breathing in it," and then attempting to participate in behavior geared towards goals (Gratz, et. al. in Baer, 2010).

The confluence of the two conceptualizations, emotional regulation, and mindfulness orientation, shows that techniques based on acceptance and awareness might enhance emotional control.

Critical, Describing and Regulating Emotions

Many people with borderline personality disorder (BPD) struggle with basic emotional regulation abilities. Marsha Linehan, a leading researcher in BPD and the creator of dialectical behavior treatment (DBT) for BPD, has proposed that feeling guideline deficits are at the root of the disorder. Recognizing how to manage your emotions is vital for everyone, whether or not you have BPD. But what exactly is a feeling guideline, and how can you increase your ability to use emotion law?

Comprehending Emotion Regulation

Every day, we all experience emotions, both happy and bad. As youngsters, most of us learn how to cope with, express, and healthily with these emotions. However, emotion management is significantly more difficult for other people, especially those with BPD. Sometimes this is due to unpleasant childhood experiences, abuse, or damage, and other times it is due to not being shown or taught how.

It is regarded as an important area of research in psychology because there is no one agreed-upon meaning of the word "emotion control." Many scientists describe feeling law as the capacity to increase or decrease your sensations as required. If you are in the middle of a work meeting and are feeling distressed, you may try to divert yourself by thinking about anything else.

Other scientists take a broader perspective of emotion regulation, seeing it as a set of characteristics that help keep your emotional system healthy, balanced, and also functioning. Given that sensations are both permanent and relative, we may learn to modify what we feel, how strong it is, when we experience it, and how we respond to it. The distinguishing feature of emotion regulation is that it happens when a goal is triggered. Goals are incredibly personal. They are the images we have in our brains of how we want things to come out. Your environment, which includes people, objects, sights, phrases, and noises, may trigger your goals in an aware or subconscious manner.

The emotional guideline defines how people control their emotions when they have them and how they experience and communicate their feelings. The psychological guideline might be automatic or regulated, conscious or unconscious, and can influence one or more stages of the emotion-creation process. The notion of psychological policy includes bad and good sentiments and how we might improve, use, and control them.

- A psychological guideline consists of three parts:

- Taking action as a result of emotions.

- Putting a stop to actions that are prompted by emotions.

- Feelings trigger modulating feedback.

The third factor is, ideally, the best way to make use of the regulatory procedures.

Every day, we are exposed to hundreds of emotional cues, most of which need some action or reply from our end. After being assaulted with countless stimuli during the day, it is normal for the mind to get engrossed in negative thoughts or unconsciously reject feelings.

The psychological policy functions as a modifier; it assists us in filtering one of the most important pieces of information and encourages us to approach it in a manner that does not cause stress or concern.

According to studies on psychological regulation, there is a significant positive association between emotion policy and anxiety management. People who are less stressed and anxious have better emotional regulation and social-emotional intelligence.

According to research, sentiments are adaptable reflexes with a profound evolutionary biology foundation. The ways we feel and interpret them have an influence on how we think, make decisions, and organize our actions in our daily lives.

For example, a person with insufficient emotional guidance strategies is more prone to fall victim to state-of-mind polarities; their actions and behavior patterns will constantly be at the mercy of their emotions.

On the contrary, a well-regulated person would have far greater balance and judgment of their moods and behaviors. Emotional law enables us to assess the emotional outcomes to embrace and avoid carefully.

When we face a provoking signal, the brain's natural response is to activate the amygdala, a mental location that handles fight-or-flight movements. Emotional policy processes help us to purchase time before acting on our fight or flight responses.

Examples of Emotion Regulation

Here are some examples of triggered aims that cause you to regulate your feelings:

- **Affecting another person's adjustment:** If you're a parent, your goal may be to help your child learn how to manage their own emotions. When your child has a meltdown, you may feel furious or amused, but instead of screaming or laughing, you control your emotions and speak quietly to your child about how they may behave instead. This is known as the exterior emotion policy.

- **Influencing a change in yourself:** If one of your goals is to be more optimistic, you may regulate your negative emotions by focusing on good ones. The self-control of emotions is referred to as "inherent emotion regulation." This kind of control is often motivated by what our society perceives as good or bad experiences or how we must behave in certain circumstances, such as during a funeral.

- **Fulfilling long-term goals:** You may also regulate your emotions to achieve another goal. For example, if your boss treats you poorly at work, you pretend it doesn't bother you since you're expecting a job promotion.

- **Changing the intensity, duration, or kind of emotions:** At times, we work to minimize or increase the intensity of our sentiments. We may also control how long our sensations linger. At times, we may alter the kind of emotion we are experiencing.

- **Subconscious regulation:** This kind of sensation policy occurs without your knowledge or awareness. An example of this would be rapidly flipping over the network when you see something upsetting on television.

In certain circumstances, these objectives overlap. You may soothe an agitated child (external) to help minimize your own rage and irritation (innate).

Most Useful Emotional Regulation Skills for Adults

Pausing between emotions and reactions is the essence of self-regulation. It encourages us to take our time and respond after honestly examining a situation. A trainee that screams at others as well as strikes his companions for petty motives surely has far less psychological control than a kid that, before yelling or beating, notifies the instructor about their concerns.

One larger aspect of emotional law is worth exploring. When we respond impulsively without paying attention to what is going on within, we often depart from our basic beliefs and behave in ways that are opposed to them. We can remain cool under pressure and avoid behaving against our basic ideals and principles via adequate legislation and self-control.

Here are several talents that may help develop emotional policy and maintain it amid difficult life situations.

Self-Awareness

Discovering and recognizing our emotions is a huge step toward emotional law. When you're feeling down, ask yourself, "Am I sad, despairing, humiliated, or distressed?"

Give yourself some options and pay attention to your feelings. Try to identify the unique sensations that you are experiencing inside yourself at that very moment, and write them down if you choose. At this stage, you do not need to act or assess the origin and effect of your emotions; all you need is a complete acknowledgment of each sensation that is controlling your mind "today."

Mindful Awareness

Mindfulness allows us to examine and also decide all aspects of the outer environment, including our body, in addition to developing thought knowledge. Simple attentive techniques like breath control or sensory relaxation help calm the turmoil inside us while also directing our activity effectively.

Cognitive Reappraisal

Cognitive reappraisal is the process of changing the way we believe. It is an essential component of psychotherapies such as CBT, DBT, and Anger Management, and it requires more acceptance as well as variety.

Cognitive reappraisal skills may involve methods such as thought substitution or situational function turnarounds, in which we attempt to see a difficult circumstance from a completely different perspective.

For example, we may replace notions like "My boss hates me," "I am no longer necessary here," and so on with alternatives like "My boss is upset right now, I am certain I can compensate," or "I know I am hardworking and also honest, let me give it another go," and so on. Doing so gives us a wider and more accurate understanding of our problems, and we may react to them more positively.

Versatility

Psychological dysregulation limits our ability to respond to life interventions. We become considerably more susceptible to distractions and fail our coping strategies, which is why we often begin withstanding treatment.

Unbiased evaluation is an excellent exercise for increasing adaptability.

When you're overwhelmed with uncomfortable sensations that you want to avoid and are afraid of reacting negatively to them, take a minute to consider, "What if my ideal close buddy was experiencing the exact same thing?" "What would I have advised them to do in these circumstances?" If you wish, compose your comments and attempt to believe that you are doing the same acts for yourself!

Self-Compassion

Making time for ourselves every day is an excellent way to develop emotional policy abilities. Advising ourselves of our abilities and merits, as well as allowing our brains to settle on a variable location, might drastically alter how we respond and how we feel to our sentiments.

The following are some easy self-compassion hacks:

- Positive self-affirmations on a daily basis.

- Relaxation as well as breath control.

- Meditation on compassion.

- Regular self-care.

- Journaling on gratitude.

Emotional Support

Psychotherapists believe that most of us have an intrinsic capacity to establish a long-lasting emotional repertoire and keep our psychological strength from being engaged in unpleasant ideas. We may seek emotional support inside ourselves by exercising conscious self-awareness, or we can seek help from others by engaging in satisfying relationships.

It's OK to consult a therapist or expert when our own coping mechanisms fail; the goal is to build a positive psychological shield to manage our emotions and bring out the best in us.

CHAPTER 8

Advanced Emotion Regulation Skills

Emotions Define Our Ultimate Goal

In today's environment, our emotions have an impact on our ultimate aims. The brain internalizes signals that in order to be happy, we must be successful, flawless, wealthy, and so on. Everything that does not fit into this equation is a failure. Anything less than perfection is a danger.

We cannot rely on our brains to distinguish between actual and imagined dangers and rewards. Worrying about a future situation or environment can make you feel as scared as if a tornado were coming at you. Because of these changes, our emotions are triggered many times a day and throughout our lives by things that may not deserve the emotional response we give. To really grasp the significance of emotions, we must first understand what they are, what they signify, and, most importantly, how to control them.

Learning to Quieten Your Emotions

Our emotions may sometimes swing between dangerous extremes. We are filled with wrath because we are so angry. We are overjoyed; we are in a state of happiness.

Like any other part of life, emotions must be stirred up in a reasonable and balanced way. This doesn't mean you can't jump for joy and party all week if you get into college or just have fun and forget about work for a week when you're on vacation. You just want to eat, sleep, surf, and repeat. It also does not exclude you from feeling hatred and resentment when the system violates your rights or sadness and pain when a loved one dies. Your emotions are legitimate at moments like these, on both ends of the spectrum.

It becomes a problem when these emotions are widespread in regular life. You become irritated and outraged at the least thing, or you are joyful and overly optimistic even when the circumstances do not warrant it. The thing that worries me the most is those bad feelings like envy, hatred, resentment, anger, and jealousy are triggered for no good reason. The more you respond impulsively and allow these emotions to govern you (and this isn't because you have BPD, ADHD, or any other mental disease), the more these emotions will grow like weeds and damage you mentally and emotionally, producing problems in your relationships.

You become someone who is difficult to deal with, always angry and aggressive and has difficulty establishing and retaining relationships. The problem is that none of these folks were born this way. They just let their emotions run wild; no one intervened to warn them that what they were doing was unhealthy until they became inbred with their feelings on a regular basis. So, how can you control your emotions, particularly in stressful situations? Here are six tips/exercises to help you learn to regulate your emotions and reclaim your sanity:

Do Not React Immediately

Responding to stimuli too quickly can only lead to regret. Acting on your triggers is not just a terrible error; it also leads to greater friction. STOP and pause for 5 minutes before responding to a trigger. Breathe in and out for 5 minutes. This will help your heart rate return to normal, and your muscles will relax. Look around you to discover who is in your local vicinity. Examine your surroundings and the people in them. Is it worthwhile to respond, and if so, how? Do you believe that these individuals will accept your behavior? When you get more relaxed, just tell yourself that these sensations are only temporary.

Get Guidance

Advice may be obtained in a variety of ways. It might be via treatment, through friends, or through supernatural intervention. Faith is a saving grace for many of us, particularly in our darkest times. Having a strong connection to your religion, whether through supernatural help or self-belief, is important for getting through problems in life. When you believe in yourself or in faith, you also think that life tells you what you need to accomplish and teaches you things via the people you meet and the situations you encounter. When you are feeling too much, close your eyes and picture a good outcome or point of view. The universe will reveal the best path ahead.

Finding a Healthy Outlet

Controlling your emotions entails healthily releasing any pent-up emotions. It would help if you had a healthy outlet for it, and everyone has their own manner of doing so. You may chat with friends or family members you trust, or you can go to a therapist. Hearing what others have to say might sometimes widen your perspective and knowledge. This means, of course, that you need to be open to changes, positive feedback, and ideas for making things better. Exercise is another technique to release emotions, while meditation improves your mental state.

Seeing the Bigger Picture

Everything that occurs in our life leads us to a greater purpose. Wisdom is the ability to look at what happened in the past and figure out what it means for the present. It may not make sense at first, but as time passes, knowledge will dawn on you, and you will finally see the broader jigsaw of life making sense. Maintain faith and believe that there is a reason why things happen the way they do throughout an emotionally painful incident.

Replacing Your Thoughts

Negative emotions and bad ideas are both part of a negative pattern loop. When presented with difficult events or an emotion that causes you to feel or think anything negative, replace your thoughts with something else. This is something you must force yourself to do. You need to think about other good options or the best way to handle the situation at hand.

Forgiving Your Emotional Triggers

Emotional triggers may take many forms. It might be a person, a scenario, or even a song. When you smell the fragrance of freshly made bread, it may bring back memories of the moment you had to let go of your work. Maybe you will experience a surge of rage when a coworker begins chatting with everyone in the room. You must move away or distance yourself from these ideas whenever you sense or see these triggers. Detach yourself from envy, wrath, self-loathing, and any other bad feelings.

CHAPTER 9

Basic Interpersonal Effectiveness Skills

Interpersonal efficacy refers to one's capacity to engage with others. It includes all of the abilities you use to:

- Take care of your connections.

- Keep a healthy balance of priorities and obligations.

- Balancing your "shoulds" with "wants."

- Create a feeling of self-esteem and mastery.

Why Are Interpersonal Effectiveness Skills Important?

DBT regards interpersonal skills as a crucial therapy component since they teach us how to communicate with others. The quality of our social life is determined by how we communicate with others, which significantly impacts our general well-being, self-confidence, and self-esteem. As a result, the primary objective of DBT is interpersonal effectiveness. In fact, it is taught as the second basic skill module in DBT sessions, with a wealth of tools and materials devoted to helping clients improve their interpersonal skills.

To assist clients in creating contact with others, they are taught specific techniques that allow them to engage in ordinary conversations more calmly and deliberately rather than speaking impulsively due to stress or upsetting emotions. Although there are many skills connected with communication and relationships, DBT primarily concentrates on two:

- The ability to request what you need or want.

- When appropriate, the ability to refuse requests.

Dialectical behavior therapy uses many acronyms to assist clients in learning the skills associated with each kind of effectiveness. DEAR MAN is the acronym of choice for objective effectiveness.

Using Objectiveness Effectiveness (D.E.A.R. M.A.N.)
D—Describe

Use just facts to describe the occurrence. Emotions should not be used. If you use emotions, make it seem like a police report. "The patient seemed to be unhappy."

If you speak in the third person, it will sound more like a police report. But do not use this behavior in real life. That's simply perplexing. Make no request or "dry beg." "I truly need thirty dollars" or "Oh, that cake looks nice" are examples of dry pleading. I hope I can have some." "Yes." is the finest answer to dry beggars. You do." It might also be, "Yes, it is." If they truly want it, they'll approach it like an adult. Assume you come from a religious home, and your adolescent refuses to attend church. "I've observed you don't enjoy church," you may say. "Let's talk about the advantages of remaining at home." This is crucial so that the other person knows the issue before you ask questions, request, or make an executive decision.

E—Express

Use "I feel" or other "I" expressions to express yourself. These remarks assist the speaker in taking responsibility and prevent the listener from instantly falling into defensive mode. Let us return to the example of the adolescent who stayed home from church. "I feel like you should believe what I believe, but I know you're your own person, apart from me, and I can't push my ideas on you," you could remark. I'd want you to join us at church because I'm concerned you won't be productive at home."

This is necessary so that the other person understands your point of view when you express your feelings about the circumstance you've just detailed.

A—Assert

Assert your stance by either immediately asking for what you need or explicitly explaining your viewpoint. Don't mince words, avoid euphemisms, and don't dither to the point of losing the other party's attention. To continue with the example, let us state our options for our hypothetical adolescent. "I realize that you don't want to go to church with us, and you're old enough to remain at home by yourself. Therefore, if you choose to remain at home instead of going to church, you will cook supper, set the table, have everything ready for us to eat when we return, and make plenty in case we have unexpected visitors. If you are unable to do this work, and so be helpful for the whole family while we are in church, you will return with us, even if you do not believe it."

This is significant because ambiguity leads to misinterpretation in relationships, which is the most common source of conflict. Make no ambiguity. Establish limits right now. If you're making a request, it should be clear, maybe even legalistic.

"May I please borrow your automobile from Sunday until Tuesday?" you could ask. I'll have it back by 7:00 p.m. with a full petrol tank and a clean car."

Further restrictions may be imposed by the opposing party. "Yes, but it overheats, so don't travel above 55 mph or more than 55 miles away," for example. And my license is expired, so avoid the police. Maybe get it renewed for me." In such an instance, you may say something like, "You know what? I'll take the bus. But thank you."

R—Reinforce

Make sure the other party understands why they should accept your request or agree to your terms without a battle. "Because I said so" is not an acceptable excuse. Most individuals automatically reciprocate.

"You get to remain home from church on the condition that you be productive at home," you may offer. It's a win-win situation for both of us since you don't like church, and I don't enjoy cooking after church."

In the case of the automobile, it can sound like this: "I truly need to go to a different city for a few days, but I can't hire a car because of (XYZ), so I'll have your car tested for you, and if I can afford to remedy the overheating issue, I will. If not, I'll check if anybody else is willing to part with their automobile for a few days or come up with another alternative." In all cases, the other person may plainly see that accepting your proposal has nothing to lose and everything to gain.

This is significant since reciprocity is the foundation of all relationships. It's hardly a huge problem if one side feels slighted every now and again. Yet, if one partner feels slighted on a regular basis, the relationship will most certainly terminate.

M—Mindful (Stay)

Maintain your attention on the discussion. They have no incentive to listen to you if you're responding to a text. If they're responding to a text, you do not influence it, but you may focus on the discussion rather than what they're doing. If they get defensive, consider what you may have said incorrectly and apologize, even if it's merely to get them back on track.

This is critical since it is all too easy to go off course and lose concentration, particularly in an awkward circumstance when the opposing side may be attempting to create a fight. You have a lower chance of receiving what you want if you go off on tangents, whether it's to sing and dance because someone mentioned a song lyric, to quarrel, or because one of you noticed a squirrel, particularly if you're the one chasing squirrels or singing and dancing.

Your kid may stop you from informing you that they've been skipping church with their Sunday School mates every week anyhow, so there's no use in attending. You may need to repeat yourself a few times, particularly if you're allowing them to remain at home as long as they're productive since they may not believe what they're hearing.

Repeat yourself as needed, and if you have a real child, you've probably already done so this morning. Then return the discussion to the issue. Detour…focus. In the case of asking an adult buddy for anything, you don't have the same power as a parent. You may still need to repeat yourself, but the interruptions may be singing and dancing.

You may say something like, "I realize you don't enjoy church, and you cut Sunday School anyhow. But if you keep going, you'll get something out of it every week, which I'd appreciate." Alternatively, "If you're going to remain home, you'll need to cook for us, and I'll take the further precaution of changing the Wi-Fi password every Saturday to make sure you'll be productive. I'll stop

doing that if you can show that you are, that you don't
have guests over, that you cook and clean as you go."

A—Appear Confident

Regardless of how you really feel, you seem confident.
Little elderly women will ask you for a napkin at a res-
taurant while you're on a date if you wear this look all
the time, and it may not even occur to you to tell them
you don't work there, so you stroll into the kitchen and
get the napkins.

Your nonverbal signals convey greater confidence than
your vocal indications. Sit up straight with your back
straight and your head held high. Establish direct eye
contact. Turn your feet in the direction of the other
person. Where your feet point is where your mind travels
unconsciously. Stand your ground and seem confident.

This is significant because confidence indicates that your
request is not too tough to grant and that you are more
difficult to reject. There's no need to be obnoxious. If
they decline, in an adult-to-adult chat, you may just ask
if they're sure, thank them for their time, and move on.

If your adolescent refuses, this is a good moment to
inform them of the alternative. "All right, you don't have
to learn to cook. By the way, if you can read, you can

cook. You are welcome to continue attending church with us, and I appreciate your informing me of the cancellation of Sunday School. I'll be sure to inform your friends' parents, since they'll be curious as well. I'll inform them that you informed me. Thank you for being concerned about the salvation of your friends, who should also return to church." This will almost certainly guarantee you a wonderful supper every Sunday.

N—Negotiate

Negotiate. Remember, "give to gain," as self-serving as it may appear. "What's in it for me?" everyone asks. You are not requesting anything. You're requesting something or establishing a rule. Even while establishing regulations, you are not demanding. Expect defensiveness and conflict if you believe you can demand anything from someone, even a youngster. Provide alternatives.

You may need to revise your request to make it more appealing. In the vehicle-borrowing scenario, you promised to have the automobile diagnosed (AutoZone does it for free) and repaired if possible, and if not, you'd find another solution to your issue.

This is significant because, although it may or may not be the essential reason we spend a few decades in this world, it definitely consumes most of our time. We spend an unusual lot of time with other people or thinking about them, whether we know them personally or not, whether we spend that time in genuine connections with other people or wondering why we push other people away.

Therefore, browbeating people and expecting them to grovel to us works only if you have money, and even then, not everyone loves you, even if you win elections. Ordinary people who don't have enormous amounts of money can't act like that. We must bargain and play nice.

CHAPTER 10

Advanced Interpersonal Effectiveness Skills

Using Relationship Effectiveness (G.I.V.E.)

The DBT acronym for establishing and sustaining relationships is GIVE. This is challenging for many individuals, but especially for those suffering from mental problems.

G—(be) Gentle

While addressing others, be courteous. We seem to be considerably more capable of being good to total strangers and individuals we work with (but don't really like) than we are of being kind to those we love. Whenever you need to discuss a sensitive subject with a loved one, be aware of your tone of voice, facial expressions, body posture, and other nonverbal indications that we all convey every day.

Accept NO as a response from the DEAR MAN method. Remember, this is a discussion between adults, not your fictitious youngster. Individuals have the right to refuse without being judged, guilted, misled, or begged. Please don't quit the conversation, and don't threaten or manipulate them.

Don't threaten to harm them, another person, or yourself. If you actually feel the need to self-harm while chatting with them, apologize for attempting to initiate the conversation, leave the situation, and get treatment.

Don't call them names, belittle them, or bring up prior hurts or "debts" you believe they owe you. No matter what you've done in the past, they don't owe you the right to say yes. If this is a one-sided relationship, you should reconsider how much time and energy you put into it. Don't use guilt or push the subject.

Thank you for your time. At the right moment, leave the situation or change the topic. Remember, no one owes you anything, and you owe nothing to anybody. Be considerate. Once they say no, use your inner voice and return to being friends. You've reached adulthood. You are capable of resolving this issue.

I— (act/be) Interested

The instruction instructs you to seem interested in what the other person has to say, yet, you should be interested. Anybody may pretend to be interested. You're undoubtedly reading this with interest right now. Yet, you must be engaged in dialogues with loved ones, even unpleasant discussions such as those necessitated by a DEAR MAN attitude. They're going to say something that will be relevant later in the dialogue.

Take an interest. Pay attention. Take caution. Show them the same interest you would want to see displayed to you. Your comments, deeds (or inactions or silence) should not invalidate their statements. Let them feel heard. Instead of waiting to speak, please pay attention to what they're saying. Worst, don't interrupt them while they're speaking.

Use open-ended inquiries to demonstrate that you're paying attention. Please take note of your body language and make sure it's welcoming and demonstrating interest, such as nodding. Keep eye contact. When you speak, be sure you're not solely talking about yourself. Make room for others in the discourse. Be at ease with stillness. It's just fine.

Consider the wants of the other person. If they want to discuss anything else, ensure this issue is finished, and all sides are happy. If you haven't arrived yet, let them know you'd be pleased to discuss it later.

V—Validate

Let the other person express their emotions. It would help if you did not tell people how they should or should not feel. When they make strong arguments, don't tell them they're simply talking like a debater, as if it invalidates their case. Don't discount what they have to say because they are younger or haven't experienced your experiences. Even if you disagree with their argument, let them know you understand where they're coming from. "I completely see why you're thinking that now. Thank you for stating things so clearly. I still don't agree, but I'll quit attempting to persuade you."

Determine whatever portion of your request makes the other person uncomfortable. "I understand you're busy, but I'm not in a hurry." "I didn't realize your automobile was such a shambles, and that's why you work from home," for example. I'll find a method to hire an automobile."

Even in the absence of confrontation, this is a vital inter-personal skill to master. Everyone enjoys being affirmed and heard. Everyone wants to feel important in a relationship. One of the most important aspects of trusting relationships is validating others.

E— (use an) Easy Manner

Smiling goes a long way in talks, whether they are heated or not. A genuine grin, not the forced "I genuinely want to murder you" smile. That grin is usually false until you've been in customer service for at least a decade. You're a natural if you have. You can fool the greatest human liar detectors with phony grins.

A sense of humor might also help. If your joke goes flat, blame it on your father. "It was one of my father's worst jokes. In fact, it may have been his greatest. He works as an accountant." You are joking if you say something serious and everyone looks at you strangely. "I'm joking! Why are you staring at me like that? I'm joking!"

Make a genuine compliment. If you can't think of one, tell them you're envious of their lack of a criminal record. You were joking about not having a follow-up tale for why you'd say that. You were joking when they looked at you like that. Use self-deprecating humor to brighten the situation. That stuff is incredible. If nothing else, just smile, nod, and pay them more attention. Make them feel important.

Self-Respect Effectiveness (F.A.S.T.)

FAST is about retaining one's dignity in the face of confrontation. You may have been a doormat for far too long. You may have the position of the youngest, the "baby," and so be treated as such regardless of your age. Even late in the game, set appropriate limits. Preserve your dignity. You can do this even with self-deprecating humor if you've established healthy limits. It would be best if you practiced these abilities sequentially, then all at once.

F—Fair

Be honest with yourself and others. A borderline personality disorder is often associated with anxiety and sadness (mental diseases are like potato chips—you can't have just one). One of the anxiety's favorite pastimes is to make every decision, action, response, and event totally awful, apocalyptic, and irreversible. It's a lot of fun. Here's a tip: label your nervousness. Make use of a fictitious character you despise. Using a genuine person you despise will enhance your uneasiness. As these ridiculous end-of-the-world scenarios begin to form, say, "Umbridge, go away." Or whatever you want to call it. It allows you to remove yourself from the anxiety and see that you are not freaking out, but your anxiety is.

Be fair in both your ideas and your deeds. Instead of believing the other person is the worst person on the globe or that you are the stupidest person ever born, switch your thoughts to something more equitable, then return your attention to the matter. Identify the truth factors in their argument; if you can't, ask clarifying questions. Please get to the point where their point of view makes sense to you. You don't have to agree with it, but you now understand it and may even agree with some of its points.

A—(no) Apologies

This isn't to imply you shouldn't apologize when you're wrong. When you're in the wrong, apologize profusely. This does not imply that you should not apologize when you are not at fault. A normal lady is a good illustration of this. She'll say "Sorry" instead of "Excuse me" or "On your left" as she passes you.

While settling a disagreement with someone, you may be tempted to apologize just to get it over with and take responsibility when it does not belong to you. Keep your dignity. Please don't do it. Don't even try to make a phony "I'm sorry you feel that way" apology. Ask open-ended questions such as "Why do you feel that way?" or "What responsibilities do you believe you have in this scenario?" without assigning blame or becoming defensive.

S—Stick to Your Values

To adhere to your principles, you must first understand what they are. Before beginning this conversation, consider your ideas. Conduct some introspective self-examination to determine what is essential to you, what you will not compromise on, and what you can compromise on without losing respect for yourself. You are the only one who has to live in your thoughts. Make sure that individual is someone you can respect and adore.

Be truthful about what you claim your values are and what they are. If you claim you value economic responsibility but never budget, you should either start budgeting or stop saying you do. You should reconsider if you profess you respect family and cheat on your wife. It could assist in writing out your values and then writing down the activities you do to support those ideals. This may assist you in determining your values. Keep standing after you've decided what you stand for.

T—(be) Truthful

Be honest with yourself and others. Do you overstate your triumphs while downplaying your flaws? So you minimize or ignore your flaws while exaggerating your achievements? Do you accept credit or blame for something that belongs to someone else? This is unnecessary in the adult world. If you can be honest with yourself, others will see you as more honest. Are your statements true? Will your interpretation of a tale be closely like that of others?

Are you as objective as possible in your assessment of yourself and others? You may keep your dignity by following these procedures. You may not be satisfied with the conversation's conclusion, but you may leave with your head held high.

Exposure-Based Cognitive Rehearsal

During cognitive therapy, the psychiatrist assists you in tracking, analyzing, and changing patterns of thought that contribute to anxiety. In certain circumstances, these reasoning modes entail overestimating the risk of harm. For example, if you are frightened of public speaking, you may overestimate your chances of being insulted, penalized, or blamed if you speak in front of others. If you're terrified of spiders, you could overestimate the likelihood that a spider would spring up and bite you if you go too close. Convinced that danger lies around the corner, you may get terrified and nervous in several settings. Certain cognitive habits in CBT include feelings that you are unable to cope with anxiety-provoking circumstances (that you are actually unable to cope with or that it would be too much for you to cope with), tragic thoughts (that things will end horribly, such as going to a party, where people may ask you why you came and urge you to leave), and others. According to CBT, any of these thinking patterns will increase your anxiety. Therapists often utilize cognitive therapy in CBT to assist you in learning how to change your thinking habits to generate more helpful or realistic thoughts.

Exposure and Response Prevention

You may not like the thought of exposing yourself to the same things that cause anxiety, obsessions, or panic attacks. Don't go just yet; hear me out. Exposure and response prevention is all about exposing oneself to triggers and having them be useful. My first interaction with this CBT approach had me dressed in my running shoes. It was not something I was willing to put myself through. You've definitely had the same notion, but take a moment to consider how this might help you recover and find peace.

The Exposure part of Exposure and Response Prevention (ERP) implies that you expose yourself to items, pictures, circumstances, and thoughts that ruffle your feathers, making you worried and anxious and bringing up all your obsessions. The second component of ERP, Reaction Prevention, requires you to resist all the ruffling and stay calm even after all the triggers have been activated. This may seem frightening, especially given how our triggers bring out the worst in us.

Consider such triggers to be warning bells. When an alarm sounds, it draws your attention and signals that it is time to act. For example, if your security alarm goes off while you are asleep, you know there is an intruder and should notify the police, even if your cat has set it off. Whatever sets off the alert, we all react similarly, wanting to protect ourselves and our families.

Similarly, these triggers are intended to draw your attention, almost as a warning, and to prepare you for whatever is to come. Nevertheless, with mental diseases, the triggers seem to be a threat and cause us to respond obsessively. You don't even have time to examine if it's a true break-in or a bat that landed on the window and set off the alarm. We often enable any trigger, no matter how little, to sound like seven shooters smashed through the door with weapons blazing. Most of the time, the triggers you enable to keep your hostage are little, but you make them seem terrible and scary. You may discover that when the alarm sounds, it conveys danger rather than alerting you to the fact that there is a possible hazard.

Naturally, deciding to begin the ERP approach may be tough since it seems like you are purposefully exposing yourself to risk. Nevertheless, using ERP, you will be able to modify the way your brain functions. Have you ever discovered that most of the time, when you believe you are in danger, you are not? When you cannot regulate your responses, you assume the worst and act accordingly. Beginning your ERP journey will assist you in gaining control of your thoughts and emotions and hence your behavior. While the beginning is certain to be difficult, it is better to begin with, a trained therapist. After a time, you'll find it simple to handle ERP on your own.

Is It Effective?

Before you subject yourself to what looks to be a pain, which I promise you are not, you may be wondering whether it is worthwhile. Certainly, the effort is worthwhile. ERP has been shown in several trials to be helpful, especially in the long-term treatment of OCD and anxiety. Unlike medicine, which causes symptoms to resurface after the prescription wears off, the benefits of ERP success continue beyond the therapy. Moreover, the

Emotional Processing Theory states that the ERP therapy technique contains profound teachings.

How Does It Work?

Two cognitive theories best describe how ERP works: the inhibitory-learning model and the habituation-learning model.

Individuals acquire diseases mostly due to misinterpreting the importance of naturally occurring intrusive thoughts that we all encounter at various stages in our lives. Additionally, having dysfunctional ideas, such as overestimation of threat, the quest for perfection, a need to regulate thoughts, and an inflated feeling of duty for the protection of self and others, all feed OCD by making intrusive thoughts seem substantial and dangerous.

By exposing you to the stimuli, ERP helps to confirm those incorrect views. If you have a severe dread of crossing highways as you anticipate getting knocked down, then continually having to cross a road and not getting knocked down can remove that anxiety. Moreover, ERP breaks down the conditioned response that you have between obsessions and compulsions.

Inhibitory-Learning Model

Unlike habituation, the inhibitory-learning model of ERP posits that the relationship between the obsession/stimuli and the fear persists and does not dissolve. Instead, exposure to the stimuli introduces new inhibitory linkages and safety-based associations. The model's goal is to teach patients that their feared consequences may occur when they are exposed to the stimuli but can also occur when they are not. As a result, individuals must acquire cognitive and emotional flexibility to prepare for and cope with whatever event occurs.

In essence, you learn to be more tolerant of suffering while also being aware of what is happening around you, rather than sitting back and waiting for the homeostasis process to kick in, as in habituation. You don't sit back and wait for nature to run its course here; instead, you prepare for the potential of your concerns coming true or not. Rather than freezing and waiting for the body to attempt to stabilize, you respond to the actual circumstance and what is occurring. You invest in the now rather than a hypothetical outcome.

The inhibitory-learning paradigm assists you in developing adaptability by changing your emphasis from potential future-oriented consequences to current experiences and values. Moreover, placing you in charge offers you authority and control. You discover that you have the ability to choose where to concentrate your attention. You may concentrate on what is occurring now or future possibilities without waiting for habituation to develop. It is liberating to be able to direct your thoughts and energies.

Exposure Therapy

Exposure exercises are used in OCD behavior treatment to expose patients to feared things, such as a contaminated door handle, or dread ideas, such as a loved one dying in a vehicle accident, over and over again until their anxiety is decreased.

The exposure prevents patients from engaging in rituals or compulsions. Avoidance routines keep you from unlearning your worries and realize you have the ability to deal with the distress generated by obsessions. When you regularly expose yourself to something you're frightened of, and no bad effects arise, your fear will gradually disappear.

Exposure Therapy Requires Patience and Courage

Such exposures force you to withstand greater levels of worry for a longer amount of time than you are used to. After the temporary pain wears off, your fear will fade, and you will no longer need to participate in the rituals of avoidance that have come to define your existence.

Exposure-based treatments are easy and effective approaches to treating OCD symptoms, but they need guts and a willingness to try them.

Facing fears: Exposure and Reaction Prevention are two methods you may employ at home (ERP). ERP is performed by:

- Placing oneself in circumstances that may cause obsessions (triggers)

- Avoiding ineffective coping mechanisms (compulsions or avoidance)

Getting to Know Your OCD

To confront your concerns, you must be aware of your thoughts (your obsessions) and determine what causes your obsessions and compulsions. You may keep track of this by creating a chart at home. You may monitor the triggers on your chart every day for a week. To get a good picture of your obsessions and compulsions, note three triggers every day (one in the morning, one in the afternoon, and one in the evening).

In the "Fear" field, assess how great the fear was in the given circumstance. Employ a 0 to 10 rating scale, with

0 representing no fear and 10 representing intense terror. Then, write down all of the compulsions you employed in reaction to the fixation. Include both behavioral and mental solutions for dealing with fixation and dread.

Create a Fear Ladder

After a week of tracking your obsessions and compulsions, you are ready to make a list of everything you dread. To create a fear ladder, rank orders your triggers from least terrifying to most frightening. Going on a stroll, for example, may only elicit a dread of 1/10 in someone who is afraid of contamination. On the other hand, using the bathroom in a shopping mall may score high since it elicits a 9/10 dread.

Facing Fear One Step at a Time

By constructing a fear ladder, you will be able to confront your anxieties by exposing yourself to events that trigger your obsessions (exposure) and opposing any efforts to manage them (response prevention).

Exposure

- Bottom-up. Work your way up the fear scale, beginning with the simplest thing (for example, fear=2/10).

- Keep track of your progress. Keep note of your anxiety levels as you go through the exposure exercise to monitor the progressive decrease in your dread.

- Don't try to dodge it. If you are being exposed, redirect your attention and prevent subtle avoidance (for example, thinking about something else, chatting to someone, and tapping the doorknob with just one finger rather than all of your fingers). The longer you avoid it, the harder it will be to conquer your worries.

- Don't be in a hurry. If your fear level is at least six out of ten, you should remain in the circumstance until it falls to two out of ten. Moreover, conquer each phobia one at a time. Repeat the exposure until the first item in the hierarchy no longer gives you difficulties.

TIP: You may build a ladder to overcome any fear you have. If you are concerned about contamination, you may need to construct a different hierarchy. A second ladder may also be required for any scenarios when you dread disaster.

TIP: Getting worried throughout these workouts indicates that you're progressing!

CHAPTER 12

Learn Not to Be Overwhelmed by Painful Situations

Managing Stress Using DBT

DBT-taught Distress Tolerance skills may help you withstand stressful conditions without hurting yourself. They may not supply you with long-term ideas but teach you how to manage yourself well when things are rough. The following are some strategies for dealing with extreme stress:

Distraction

Stress might drive you to get engrossed in ruminating and worrying. Indulging your mind and body in a job that diverts your attention and keeps you from thinking about whatever is worrying you, at least for a while, may give you enough time to think about the stressor and plan how to deal with it. Distract your thoughts from the tension by calling a buddy, working out, reading your favorite book, or watching a hilarious movie.

Self-Soothe

Keep in mind to be nice and kind to yourself. It is normal to be harsh on oneself, particularly during times of stress. You assess your talents and believe you cannot deal with your challenges. Integrating calming hobbies into your daily life will help you deal with stress and anxiety. To relax your body, listen to peaceful music, make cookies, enjoy a gorgeous sunset, or eat your favorite dish.

Relax

Following the distress tolerance module necessitates relaxation exercises for both the mind and the body. Check out all of the things that will help you relax. Take a hot shower or participate in relaxation exercises. Avoid doing numerous activities at once and try to concentrate only on the present activity. Create a calming mental picture.

Ponder the Pros and Cons

Grab a piece of paper and a pen and construct two lists of the benefits and drawbacks of a difficult circumstance. Write out how stress might harm you if you don't pay attention to it. Consider how stress may help you expand and improve as a person. After you're finished, look through the lists again to inspire yourself.

Breathe

Examine your breathing pattern more attentively. To enhance your mental attention, try deep breathing or counting your breaths. This might help you relax and pay attention.

Summary

Because of constant stress, it is very simple to go down a rabbit hole and lose sight of the essential things in your life these days. Remember that you have power in every situation, even if it means letting go of things over which you have no control. You may not be able to address every difficulty in your life, but with DBT distress tolerance skills, you will be able to handle your frustrations far more confidently. Do not allow stress to overcome you!

Managing Worry Using DBT

There is no quick fix for anxiety, but there is one that genuinely works: DBT. While negative ideas might persist for a long time, you can quickly cultivate a Teflon mind. It simply takes a little effort.

Look for the Canaries in the Coal Mine

Realize that the ideas that are bothering you are just that: thoughts. This ability may take time to learn, but it is possible to embrace it rapidly. Negative emotions are more difficult to manage. These two may team up on you; unpleasant ideas lead to negative emotions and vice versa, keeping you in a horrible circle.

You tend to forget about your body when you get caught up in worrisome thoughts. Recognize the bodily sensations resulting from your emotions, such as sweat, short breathing, and muscular tension.

Make a list using a piece of paper and a pen. When you are anxious, write down everything that comes to you. Make a mental note of any bodily manifestations that occur during a stressful experience. This is referred to as locating the canaries in the coal mine. Take note of the acts you perform when you are frightened (such as procrastination, drinking alcohol, etc.). Familiarize yourself with these steps so that you will know what to do the next time anxiety hits.

Avoid Avoiding

Why should you avoid doing so? Because you must disprove your fears. If you continue to avoid triggers, you will just prolong your anxiety. Worrying and then recognizing your anxiety was pointless results in a phenomenon known as "extinction," and the worry gradually fades away.

On the other hand, ignoring what you feel repeatedly leads you to think that these things are real and that fearing them is the correct thing to do. This is known as "reinforcement," and it just adds to the anxiety.

Remember that you are mistaken if your mind tells you to avoid a situation. Let yourself cherish the moment by seeing it as an opportunity to overcome your fear and move away from your troubles. Shift your attention away from troubling ideas and onto the actual world.

Now that you've learned the most crucial thing to avoid let's move on to the one you should do.

Identify

Have you ever looked back on a worrying event and said, "Wow, that truly frightened me out?" This is due to your failure to recognize it at the time it happened. Concerns tend to creep up on you and dominate you when you go through cognitive fusion. This compels you to make poor choices. The easiest approach to avoid this issue and all the fuss it causes is to recognize the rising anxiousness before it's too late.

You should have developed your own list of canaries by now. Great. It would help if you started detecting these things as soon as they occur. The sooner you recognize these ideas, action impulses, and bodily manifestations, the sooner you will be able to stop them. If you know what you're searching for, identifying your issue is simple. This allows you to at least control or handle it.

Engage

Have you ever been overwhelmed with disturbing thoughts about a certain subject, only to have larger difficulties hit you? This new difficulty pushes you to forget about your old problems and focus all of your remaining energy on them. Take note of your ability to alter your focus. The difficult thing is doing it on purpose.

This skill is intended to assist you in developing a connection with your emotions and experiences. It will teach you how to stay in the present moment and connect with your life rather than spending your energy on negative ideas. Hence, if you find yourself in a stressful or worried situation, remember to keep your attention only on the subject at hand, avoiding any troubling thoughts that may distract you. Concentrate all of your focus on the present moment. If anxiety is distracting you, remember this point and focus only on the situation at hand, making every attempt to solve it.

Tend to Your Emotions

The first step in tending to your emotions is recognizing concern. After you've realized you're in a bad situation, pay special attention to your body. Check for any indications of your heightened emotions. You may feel your heart rate increase, your muscles tense, or your stomach drop. Pay careful attention to everything you are feeling.

Your mind may shift its focus to any other subject. You may also feel as if you're drowning in a pool of anxieties, which diverts your focus away from the real issue. Get yourself together as soon as you find yourself in this circumstance. Try returning your full attention to your body and concentrating on the genuine issue. Do not get absorbed in troubling ideas. All you have to do is notice them and keep returning your awareness to the body repeatedly. Identify your feelings, whether they be ones of dread, worry, irritability, sorrow, or embarrassment.

Tell yourself that it is natural to feel the way you are right now and that your feelings will not kill you.

To summarize, inspect, admit, and mark. The anxious sensations will gradually go. It is a talent that takes time to master but is undeniably effective. When you master it, it will become your superpower against anxiety.

Use Opposite Action

This may seem to be advanced Kung Fu, so proceed with caution. Ultimately, this technique will transform you from a chronically troubled person to someone who seldom worries. It is a gentle sort of "exposure therapy" that focuses on "confronting your anxieties."

Opposing action assists your brain in determining which persons and situations are not harmful and hence do not need to be avoided. As your brain makes this link, your anxieties begin to fade. You stop avoiding people or things and get the freedom to do and go wherever you choose in life.

Please take a minute to respond to the following questions:

- Are you concerned about things that aren't an actual or urgent threat?

- Do you worry so much that it's tough to enjoy yourself?

- Is it more probable that you will be sad than happy?

- Do you refuse to accept reasonable risks?

- Is concern interfering with your daily activities?

You are most likely healthy if you answered no to the following questions. Therefore, continue doing what you're doing since you're only alert to actual risks. You will go to any length to enjoy a happy existence.

But, you are worried if you answered no to most of the above questions. It is vital to execute the measures outlined above in order to remove the unwanted load from your shoulders and begin living.

Regrettably, no miracle medicine can instantly ease you or your troubles. As previously indicated, following DBT in a progressive manner may have a tremendous influence on your life and make it simpler for you.

CHAPTER 13

DBT Strategies for the Individual Session

In this section, I'll continue the discussion of what you need to know to conduct individual DBT sessions by examining different ways of dealing with clients, including the importance of approval.

Finally, I'll look at some sensible methods that will assist you in balancing approval with pressing clients to change. At that time, I'll discuss the relevance of goal setting and schooling, as well as a few further comments on the therapeutic relationship, including some ideas for preparing patients for the end of treatment.

Dialectics is a philosophy that seeks to comprehend the tensions and conflicts that occur inside ourselves, between us, and throughout the cosmos. We seek to synthesize and overcome these competing tendencies in dialectics to achieve better harmony in thought and behavior.

To use a basic example, many of us interpret events as either black and white or cut and dry. On the other hand, life is frequently more complicated than the all-or-nothing choices we make.

When we apply dialectics, we comprehend the relative truth on both sides, and the resulting synthesis drives us away from the extremes of black and white and into shades of gray. Then we discover the center path and/or what we had previously neglected in our thoughts, behavior, and relationships with others. This insight results in more productive behavior.

The many DBT aspects create a framework of structure and conceptualization for both the therapist and the client. It is feasible to imagine examples of DBT based on the biosocial theory and the degree of dysfunction.

These important collaborative therapeutic postures and treatment objectives rely on priorities, and goals created hierarchically based on priorities are called priorities, and these goals are considered delivery modalities. As a result, those precise actions and duties are connected, and each level addresses specified goals. After that, we sketch them one by one.

Increasing Behavioral Control

Everything is interconnected with something else. This notion emphasizes the need to address transformation from a whole-systems viewpoint. It also serves as a reminder that the client's behaviors and feelings have an effect on the therapist, who in turn has an impact on the client, and so on (Feigenbaum, 2007).

When various (perhaps contradictory) points of view are integrated, an accurate truth may be discovered (Feigenbaum, 2007). This approach contradicts the widely held belief that persons who struggle with emotion regulation perceive the world in black-and-white terms.

In other words, clients and therapists must accept the possibility of two apparently contradictory forces coexisting. As therapists and clients utilize dialectical theory, they must remember that reality is not permanent and unchanging but is in continuous change, including seeming contradictions, such as the remark that clients are putting in their best effort despite working harder and producing more.

Clients who struggle with emotion regulation, for example. Another example is the notion of being angry and loving someone simultaneously. The therapist's job is to help the client understand that they may be angry and love their partner. We must nurture acceptance while working to change things. Therapists must embrace their clients while also attempting to modify troublesome behaviors.

Yet, dialectical thinking is used in therapy in a variety of ways. This method may help therapists and clients remember to search for what is missing from their reality as they continue to seek fresh insights (Basseches, 1984).

Understanding that distinct points of view may be both correct and incorrect is a core tenet of dialectical reasoning. As you are receiving therapy, you should know that polarizations are an unavoidable part of life; having a dialectical perspective entails realizing this and being on the lookout for polarizations when they occur. The dialectical ideals of selecting the middle ground are fundamental to Zen philosophy, and DBT employs these ideas to assist clients in developing better problem-solving techniques and living happier lives.

According to previous research, the DBT model comprises four important components. Nevertheless, since most research on DBT for BPD focuses on the broader concept, it also comprises four components: people, skills training, individual treatment, and telephone consultation. I've seen DBT presented to clients in a successful manner that does not include these components.

This training group is intended to assist customers in learning and improving their abilities. This group meets once a week and is divided into four modules: basic mindfulness methods, interpersonal effectiveness techniques, emotional regulation skills, and stress tolerance techniques.

The goal of mindfulness therapy for BPD is to help patients realize their identity, but it also helps on many other levels. To properly govern their thoughts, emotions, and urges, people must become more self-aware and comprehend them better. Clients learn to tolerate undesired thoughts, emotions, and desires without acting on them, realizing that internal experiences are neither necessary nor banned and that these sensations will disappear with time.

These qualities help clients enhance their capacity to deal with interpersonal uncertainty and stress, which is common in their lives. For example, if a client has a specific goal in mind, such as maintaining or enhancing a relationship, they will be taught skills to assist them in achieving their goal.

This module's goal is to assist in lessening the chance of mood swings. Ultimately, our objective is to establish an emotional connection with our customers; thus, we offer instances such as why we hire them and why we don't want to let them leave. It is shown how linking thoughts, emotions, and actions impacts others. This lesson focuses on self-validation as well as other skills that might help clients better regulate their emotions.

These talents are also known as crisis survival skills, and they are meant to help clients get through difficult events without worsening their position by engaging in problem behaviors such as self-harm, drug addiction, and suicide attempts.

These approaches help customers relax and shift their attention away from the problem rather than toward it. Rather than focusing on the problem and acting on urges that come with unpleasant emotions, these talents let clients divert their attention elsewhere.

Individual DBT therapy sessions are usually done once a week. Therapists provide one-on-one sessions to help clients use the techniques learned in groups to reduce target behaviors such as suicide, self-harm, drug use, and so on. The structure and format utilized in group sessions will be further discussed in subsequent chapters.

The major purpose of phone consultations is to educate consumers about their own abilities. One of the purposes of phone consultations is to help clients identify the skills that would be most useful in their situation and to assist them in dealing with the obstacles that prevent them from utilizing these skills and performing successfully. DBT cannot be carried out without the assistance of others (2011). The makeup of the DBT consulting team may vary depending on the therapist's situation.

The team typically includes all therapists working in a DBT clinic, including social workers, psychologists, psychiatrists, and other therapists and personnel. This is straightforward to do since therapists usually utilize clinic settings. It is more challenging for those of us who practice in private.

Therapists who use private DBT outside of practice may choose to join forces with others to establish a team, both in practice and online, as long as confidentiality is maintained. As a private DBT practitioner, I am fortunate to get continuing consultation from a psychiatrist who works in a DBT clinic. In other words, your team does not have to be large, but you do need to get objective feedback on your practice.

Second, the team aids therapists with case discussions so that they may continue to work with clients using DBT methodologies. The team aids the therapist and ensures that DBT protocols and practices are followed while working on the case. It also helps with feelings of frustration and impotence. Team members use DBT methods such as taking a dialectical viewpoint and being nonjudgmental to prevent power disputes and other variables that might disrupt the team and the therapeutic process.

It is also critical to examine clients and assist them in assessing themselves in light of their childhood experiences. Using the biosocial paradigm in your practice may benefit clients while also preventing burnout since it reduces the need to condemn them for their actions.

CHAPTER 14

Applying DBT to Mental Health and Substance Abuse Recovery

Several critiques have been leveled regarding psychological wellness transportation in the recovery community. Therapy models are often based on the notion that there is an illustrative model for comprehending the "disarranged" person's experience.

Indeed, the more we consider the customer—their conclusion, examples of brokenness, or, in the case of DBT-WR, the nature and the extent to which the person battles with feeling guidelines—the more we can concentrate on utilizing a precise arrangement of mediations intended to neutralize the individual's dysfunctions.

Yet, the recovery process emphasizes that "it is risky to impose a model of interpretation of the (client's) insight, rather than assisting the person to establish their own translation."

Understanding what DBT is all about and having a firm concept of the DBT skills we will use to aid you is critical to acquiring a solid feel of the types of anxiety symptoms and related challenges you may have as a comprehension of what DBT is.

As a result, in this and the subsequent chapters, we will begin to present you with a road map for DBT skills. Remember how we spoke about how avoidance contributes to depression, anxiety, and other problems? In addition, in this chapter, we will introduce you to two DBT skill sets: mindfulness and distress tolerance methods, which will help you stop damaging avoidance patterns and learn to accept, tolerate, and just be attentive every second of your life, no matter how terrible things become.

This chapter will describe the many talents we discuss, how you may profit from them, and provide you with two practice projects to get you started. These and the next chapters are designed to provide you with a basic understanding of DBT skills, how they work, and what they can do for you. The next chapters contain an in-depth description of how ability may be used for specific anxiety symptoms.

By engaging in DBT mindfulness techniques, you begin to pay attention to your emotions, beliefs, and feelings in the present moment. Mindfulness, which is utilized in various treatments and has roots in both Eastern and Western religious traditions, is simply paying close attention to your present-moment experiences. Linehan 1993; Kabat-Zinn 1990.

You don't need to meditate or sit on an awful mat with incense burning in the corner to be aware; all you need is the desire to open your attention to what is happening right now.

To fully apply the other abilities described in this book, you must first be aware. Since mindfulness is all about being aware of your behaviors and emotions, it is a fundamental skill that helps you utilize your other skills.

While acquiring new skills for the first time, you must pay close attention to what you are doing and attempt to explain it to yourself. This workshop focuses on developing the other DBT tools and strategies on top of the mindfulness practice, much as a house has a core floor.

Consequently, many of our clients have said mindfulness was the most valuable skill they learned during DBT. Individuals have told us that practicing being more engaged in their daily lives may substantially transform their lives. Moreover, you will find in the next chapters that mastering mindfulness skills has some benefits.

DBT offers numerous types of attentiveness, but the basic idea is to keep your mind current and pay greater attention to your senses in the here and now. The first step toward mindfulness is frequently to pay attention to and notice your present experiences (Linehan 1993).

For obvious reasons, the next time you drink a hot beverage, whether it's hot tea, coffee, chocolate, or something else, pay attention to how it appears, its color, how it moves in the cup when you pick something up, its scent, how it feels on your tongue, the various flavors you encounter, and so on. Keep your focus on the present moment and your appreciation of your favorite warm beverage.

The idea is for you to mentally take a step back and focus on your present experience via your senses of sight, hearing, touch, taste, and smell. Keep an eye out for anything unusual. As your mind wanders, please bring it back to what you're focusing on. Don't resist, try to change, or flee what you're paying attention to. In addition to your five senses, you may observe your thoughts.

Moreover, mindfulness practice may take different forms. For example, in some ways, this is the goal of mindfulness in DBT (Linehan 1993). This approach may be used to thoroughly immerse oneself in the sipping sensation of a hot beverage.

Make this your whole attention, and fully immerse your body and mind in it. Pay attention to what you're doing and make what you're doing well the most important thing you can do. Do it with fire and enthusiasm, with your whole mind and body. Lastly, like with most other types of meditation, there are three key factors to consider while practicing DBT mindfulness skills:

- Do just one thing at a time, in the present. Avoid multitasking and juggling many tasks. Just concentrate on one activity, whether driving, eating, walking, washing the dishes, speaking with someone else, reading a book, arguing, working, or waiting.

- Make no judgments about yourself, others, or your own experiences. Use the terms "good," "bad," "right," "wrong," "should," or "should not" sparingly. If you find yourself analyzing, return your focus to the present moment or explain just the facts. Don't condemn yourself for criticizing.

- Learn from your experiences how to achieve your goals and do the things that work. Try not to squander time and energy on things that you need or want to accomplish but that, in the end, does not work for you.

As should be evident, one important benefit of care is that if you properly practice it, you will spend far more energy experiencing your life right now rather than being plagued by restless or disturbing thoughts about your past or future.

Caring, therefore, may be an antitoxin to some of the unpleasant thought patterns that individuals with anxiety commonly encounter. Subsequently, we illustrate a section of the various benefits you may notice if you exercise care abilities, including those specific to discomfort concerns and more general advantages.

A large number of people we've dealt with have mentioned these benefits, and our research also supports the notion that many people achieve at least some of them. (Baer 2003)

We hope that when we guide you through the care skills in this workout booklet, you may recognize many of these benefits in your daily living and dealing with anxiety concerns. There are several benefits to difficulty resistance abilities for people who have tension difficulties, those who are dealing with other mental or passionate obstacles, and people who do not have mental troubles. Undoubtedly, practically everyone might benefit from some experience with problem-solving talents.

These are some of the key benefits you may experience if you exercise these talents. As you go through this book, we hope you will notice these and other advantages, particularly those that will help you with anxiousness concerns. Feeling guideline skills are an important set of talents taught in DBT. These skills may help you improve your ability to control or regulate your emotions.

Specialists have defined feeling standards as to how people influence their enthusiastic moods, as well as how they experience and display their sentiments (Net 1998). Several specialists believe that concerns with emotional guidelines are a recurring feature in a variety of enthusiasm challenges and problems.

People suffering from depression, anxiety, drug abuse, character disorders, and "mad problems" (such as schizophrenia) struggle to manage their emotions. Sensing guidance talents may also be really beneficial, even if you don't have a specific emotional issue. Who among us couldn't benefit from some helpful pointers on how to control our emotions better?

To effectively manage your emotions, you must first understand what you're dealing with: what are feelings, after all? Overall, academics that study emotions acknowledge that they are a collection of reactions in the body and mind to events, memories, and contemplations (all in the same area.). Since the fabled creature, the hydra has several heads; passionate reactions have a wide variety of components.

DBT emphasizes the fact that emotions have many components and that they all operate together as one large framework, encompassing your brain, body, thoughts, and actions (Linehan 1993). As previously said, feeling guidelines are how people influence their emotions when they have them and how they experience and express them. (Net 1998).

Dealing with Difficult Times

We have experienced several hard instances previously. On occasion, our techniques for dealing with what happened were effective, and we got by OK; on other instances, we either didn't have procedures, or how we dealt with our position aggravated the problem.

The DBT emotion guideline skills help you cope with your feelings in three important ways. To begin, certain talents help you acquire, recognize, and interpret your sensations. (Linehan, 1993).

If you learn to understand and acknowledge your emotions, you may discover that they become more logical and less disturbing and frightening. Second, some talents may help you reduce your vulnerability to unpleasant or undesired sensations.

These talents often involve enhancing your own physical and enthusiastic self-care, participating in specific activities, and doing things that make you feel confident and capable (on the same page.). Lastly, some skills may help you modify and cope with your emotions.

One of these talents is learning how to step back from attention and concentrate on your emotions without avoiding or fighting them. Diverse talents include determining how to behave in a way opposite to or contradict what you want to do while experiencing a sensation (in the same place). In subsequent sections, we will show you how to use these skills to actively deal with tension and its difficulties.

As you may have seen, in order to meet our needs and achieve our goals, we must continually regulate or deal with our emotions. If you never actually deal with your emotions, you probably wouldn't be able to accomplish a lot of the activities that are important to you.

CHAPTER 15

Putting It All Together

Define Your Focus

We all want to do something, but the trouble for many is that they don't know what it is that they want to accomplish. That is why it is sometimes customary, if not natural, to begin by following societal norms. Remember that there is nothing wrong with it, particularly since some individuals find fulfillment there. On the other hand, some believe that something is missing and get irritated as a result.

Your and others' self-confidence is significantly influenced by what you regard to be your primary objective in life. Your sense of self-assurance and confidence will build as you devote all of your time and attention to the one thing you want to do.

Of course, you must know what you want to accomplish. In other words, your purpose must be distinct, thorough, and unequivocally obvious. But, if you still struggle to describe what you want to concentrate on, you may want to give the following exercise a try.

This is known as the "confidence pie" (or "confidence wheel" in certain circles). It will assist you in determining which aspects of your life you can be most confident in:

- **Step 1:** On a piece of paper, write down all the various parts of your life that you feel need you to be confident. Strive to have six to eight different components, such as family life, work, parenting, social interactions, academic life, etc.

- **Step 2:** On a scale of 1 to 10, with 10 being the optimal confidence level, score how you feel about each element of your life. Follow your instincts. Give yourself a 9 or 10 if you believe you are very confident in your successful profession. If you believe you consistently struggle with dating or social connections, give yourself a 2 or 3.

- **Step 3:** To depict your pie, draw a large circle on another piece of paper. "Slice" your pie into equal-sized pieces, each representing one of the parts of your life you've identified. Each element should be labeled appropriately.

- **Step 4:** Fill out each slice of the pie according to their score. For example, if "career" had a score of 9, 9/10 of the slice should be darkened. Shade just 2/10s if you awarded "social interactions" a 2, and so on. Make each pie stand out by using various colored inks.

- **Step 5:** Examine the visual depiction of your "life" in terms of your degree of confidence, and then evaluate what you can do to make all the slices equal. Keep the confidence pie in your diary to remind you of the parts of your life that need to be prioritized.

Turn Your Dreams into Goals

What does it feel like to look at your own confidence pie? It is hoped that it will motivate you to appreciate and develop the many elements of your life. You may even be excited to get started on how to develop objectives properly and efficiently to help you become more confident. The **SMART** model is one of the greatest techniques for doing so.

This model is an acronym that you may use to help you transform your thoughts into objectives. The model is broken into as follows:

- **"S" Specific:** Your aim should be as precise as feasible. That is the only way to become fully driven to succeed. For example, if you lack confidence in your financial situation, be specific about it. Do you wish to improve your financial situation? How much money do you believe it will take to make you feel that way? "Oh, a lot of money," you should say, not "five million dollars" (or more, of course). Then, turn this exact aim into something measurable. For example, you may write the amount on a check to yourself and pin it to your corkboard. This will serve as a reminder of your unique aim.

- **"M" Measurable:** It doesn't matter how detailed your objective is if you can't track your progress toward it. For example, the five-million-dollar example is simple to calculate since money is as countable as it gets. But let's assume you want to boost your confidence in your social relationships. Think about how it should be measured. Would it come in the form of time, such as spending one day a week with close friends? Or would you assess it in terms of quality, such as strengthening your listening skills so you can have a more meaningful discussion with your friend?

- **"A" Attainable:** There is nothing wrong with a tough objective, but it must also be feasible. In most circumstances, you may determine if your objective is feasible by laying out explicit stages that will get you closer to it. For example, if you aim to obtain $5 million to feel more financially secure and confident, consider how you will do it in a realistic (and honest) manner. You might begin by paying off all of your bills while also attempting to limit your expenditures. The next phase is raising your income while keeping a modest lifestyle. Next, you may go to savings and investments, and so forth.

- **"R" Rewarding:** You can only be driven by a goal that you believe will reward you. To put it another way, you must be able to explain "why" you desire that objective in the first place. Your response should be something that makes you excited. It is critical to remind yourself of your "why" every day so you will keep striving to achieve your objective no matter how difficult the journey may be. For example, if you want to reduce weight, consider why you would feel confident after you've done it. What counts is that your solution is gratifying enough to motivate you to commit, no matter how simple or complex it is.

- **"T" Timed:** The greatest difference between a fantasy and a goal (regardless of how detailed, quantifiable, realistic, and fulfilling it is) is a deadline. You will constantly put off your objective if you do not have one. By establishing a deadline, you are racing against the clock to accomplish your goals and obtain the confidence you have always desired.

When you've established your objectives, the following stage is to implement them. These are some measures you may take to attain your objectives:

- **Step 1:** Choose one element to concentrate on. Although you may wish to feel more confident in numerous areas of your life, tackling them one at a time is best. You won't feel as overwhelmed this way. As you observe yourself improving in one area, you may shift your attention to the next. It is good to begin with, the component that you cherish the most.

- **Step 2:** Make a goal statement out of your focus statement. As a guide, use the SMART model.

- **Step 3:** Create a thorough strategy to take you through the action steps. It might take the form of a step-by-step plan, a schedule, or a checklist. Make changes to your strategy until you are satisfied with it.

- **Step 4:** Keep track of your progress and any set-backs. Make any required changes. Remember that your comprehensive strategy should not be finalized. It should, instead, enable you to respond to unanticipated developments. If you believe in your aim, you will have the confidence to roll with the punches.

- **Step 5:** Maintain progress and adapt to changes. Consider failures to be chances to pivot to a new path. You will eventually discover the appropriate way that will bring you to your destination.

Find a Confidence Mentor

Confidence, believe it or not, can be infectious. When you surround yourself with confident individuals who encourage others to believe in themselves, it's natural for you to want to be like them. On the other hand, spending too much time with negative individuals can drive you to be more judgmental of yourself and others.

It's simple to suggest that you pick friends that build you up and help you discover confidence in yourself, but not everyone can do so. If you're still working on being confident enough to meet new people, finding a mentor is the greatest method to be inspired by others.

They may be a public person you respect who frequently makes video blogs on YouTube or writes uplifting articles online, for example. Apart from receiving frequent updates from these mentors, you may also read autobiographies of individuals who overcame difficulties to accomplish great things. Make time each day to read, listen to, or watch someone who inspires you, even if it is just for five minutes.

How to Be the Main Character in Your Life

In the 2006 film The Holiday, an insecure, disturbed girl called Iris (played by Kate Winslet) meets a retired but brilliant Hollywood filmmaker named Arthur (played by Eli Wallach). When she told him she was still in love with her ex-boyfriend despite the fact that he was already engaged to another woman, he offered her some sound advice.

Many individuals go through life without developing good personal standards. They end up being the sidekick in their own life when they deserve to be just as remarkable, courageous, honorable, and as astute as the main character. Although it goes without saying that real life isn't like the movies, it doesn't mean you can't be "The One" who saves the day.

How can you develop the courage to become the major character in your own life? What you will do is as follows:

- **Step 1:** Decide to make a positive change. You have control over your life, not your family, friends, or employer. Realize that you will be your continuous friend in this life. Although your connections are vital, your own ideas, actions, and choices are all you actually have. As you decide to accept responsibility for yourself, you will notice a significant shift in your viewpoint.

- **Step 2:** State clearly what you want to accomplish in life. Say it out loud to yourself, whatever aim you have in mind. You are announcing to yourself and the universe that you are embarking on a journey to achieve a goal. This objective will make you feel as though you have had a wonderful life on this planet.

- **Step 3:** Get started! Prepare a specific plan and work with what you have. Every day, learn something new, bearing in mind that errors and failures are among the finest instructors. Good friends should be treasured and supported. Get advice from your mentors. Most importantly, don't take the current moment for granted since you can never go back in time.

Know what you want and take the reins of your own journey to get it. Spend time each day motivating yourself and staying on track. Most importantly, enjoy yourself. Confidence will quickly come if you concentrate on and act on what you genuinely value in life.

CHAPTER 16

Frequently Asked Questions

How Are CBT and DBT Different?

DBT is based on CBT; however, it takes a more dialectical approach than typical CBT treatments. While most individuals may obtain substantial outcomes from CBT, it was discovered that a particular subset of patients was not getting the same results as the ordinary person. Instead, this group became dissatisfied with the process and swiftly left out due to a lack of validation. As a result, a redesigned CBT procedure was created that blends emotional affirmation with behavioral modification. This is referred to as DBT.

Are CBT and DBT More Effective Than Other Therapies?

These treatments have been clinically demonstrated to be very successful, and most customers see immediate and long-lasting results. All treatments have advantages; however, cognitive-based therapies are often favorites among physicians since they are action-oriented, resulting in faster outcomes. Most individuals can get the same effects in 3 to 4 sessions of CBT or DBT as they would in a year of talk therapy.

How Does the Therapy Work?

The quantity of treatment required varies according to your own requirements; however, most individuals do well with one individual session each week. DBT also includes one extra weekly skill-building group session. Your dedication to the therapeutic process is the most important determinant of how well the therapy will work. Some individuals have more than one individual session every week, while others are content with only one. It is something you should address with your therapist in order to develop a customized treatment plan.

How Long Does It Take to See Progress?

Individual progress varies, but most individuals experience effects relatively quickly, usually within 3 to 4 sessions. Of course, this heavily depends on how much work you put into the software. Completing your homework regularly and attending the weekly group skill-building sessions are important to your success in DBT. Several of the skills you will learn throughout therapy are included in this book.

What If I'm Skeptical?

Could you give it a go? You won't know whether it works till you try it. You won't know how successful it is unless you try it, just like practically everything else in life. Commit to doing your first behavioral experiment and observe the results. If it works, that's fantastic; keep going. You can always quit if it doesn't.

Can I Discontinue Medication?

While both CBT and DBT are effective therapy modalities even without medication, discontinuing your medication should be done with caution and under the supervision of a medical expert. You should consult with your psychiatrist or another physician about your choice.

How Does DBT Prioritize Treatment Goals?

- **Target 1:** conduct that endangers one's life or interferes with therapy.

- **Target 2:** Lessened emotional distress.

- **Target 3:** The third goal is to manage one's everyday life.

- **Target 4:** a feeling of belonging and completeness.

This is the most important aim of DBT therapy. Of course, life-threatening aims take precedence, and dealing with suicidal thoughts or self-harm conduct comes first. Furthermore, of great concern is conduct that interferes with treatment since no progress can be accomplished until there is a commitment to the therapeutic process. The ultimate objective is to bring you to a state of total completeness. You are one of many people in the cosmos and globally related to everyone else. Despite your religious or spiritual convictions, the ultimate purpose of DBT is to assist you in accepting yourself, your life, and other people so that you may fully experience and appreciate life.

Is Eastern Philosophy an Underpinning of DBT?

DBT's primary mindfulness component stresses remaining in the present moment and is based on Eastern traditions. The idea is to assist you in remaining in the present moment with your thoughts and emotions since events in the past or concerns about the future cause most disruptions. The Eastern world has practiced the tradition of focussing on the here and now for millennia, whereas the Western world has just lately accepted the mindfulness philosophy. It has been really beneficial for folks who sincerely want to become unstuck and no longer feel overwhelmed by their emotions.

Conclusion

Dialectic behavioral therapy is a style of psychotherapy that focuses on the interaction of emotions, events in our environment, and cognition. It acknowledges that different people can have different reactions to the same event and focuses on assisting clients in "connecting with their thoughts and taking control of them" by mastering four skills: mindfulness, distress tolerance, emotional regulation skills, and interpersonal effectiveness. According to the idea behind dialectic behavioral therapy, emotional pain is the emotional poison at the foundation of many psychological issues. DBT training employs trauma-focused cognitive-behavioral approaches to assist clients in identifying and processing their emotions, successfully regulating their moods, learning to take responsibility for their thoughts and actions, and developing strategies for coping with life's obstacles.

Therapists practice dialectic behavioral therapy; nevertheless, its theoretical foundation is held by other thinkers. Dialectic behavioral therapy differs from other treatments in that it focuses on how individuals perceive their emotions and ideas, while cognitive-behavioral therapy (CBT) and interpersonal therapy do not. Cognitive therapists concentrate on the influence of these events on behaviors, while dialectical therapists concentrate on emotional processing before the behavior.

Dialectical behavior therapy is more than simply a treatment method. Dialectical training is a method of interaction that incorporates skill development, worksheets, and set point activities. DBT teaches three major skills: mindfulness, distress tolerance, and emotional regulation. These abilities are critical to the success of this treatment. They enable individuals to learn new things, modify their behaviors, and experience the world in new ways.

Positive life experiences are emphasized in dialectic behavioral treatment. Assertiveness training, self-care skills, self-esteem growth, and connection-building are all part of this treatment. DBT is extremely similar to other kinds of psychotherapy, yet it specifically focuses on advantages that can be acquired via emotions. Dialectic behavioral therapy allows the individual to develop skills that will improve their life.

Individuals may learn more about their feelings on a daily basis. This form of treatment benefits everyone, not just those suffering from mental illnesses. It also teaches how to recognize thoughts and emotions in order to combat them before they spiral out of control. Dialectical behavioral therapy also focuses on the development of skills that might help individuals regulate their emotions, such as anger management. This is an essential component of effective living and may assist persons suffering from mental illnesses in regaining control of their life. This style of therapy teaches individuals how to make adjustments in their daily lives based on what they learn about emotions, thoughts, and behavior.

Emotional management techniques may be used to improve mental health issues. Dialectical behavioral therapy teaches patients how to deal with their emotions in various ways. This may assist persons with mental health disorders, which often include intense emotions, in using the appropriate coping mechanisms. Every individual has a unique set of feelings and ideas. As a result, every person should be taught how to utilize dialectical behavioral therapy to their advantage.

www.ingramcontent.com/pod-product-compliance
Lightning Source LLC
LaVergne TN
LVHW010339200726
843507LV00010B/1559